FATHER PEYTON'S
ROSARY PRAYER BOOK

Servant of God Father Patrick Peyton, CSC

Father Peyton's Rosary Prayer Book

The family that prays together stays together

IGNATIUS PRESS SAN FRANCISCO

Original edition © 1953, 1954, 1980,

1991, 1996, 2000 and 2001

by The Family Rosary, Inc.

Original edition published by

Holy Cross Family Ministries

518 Washington Street

North Easton, MA 02356-1200

800-299-PRAY

Cover design by The Family Rosary, Inc.

© 2003 The Family Rosary, Inc.

Revised 2005

Published in 2003 Ignatius Press, San Francisco

ISBN 978-0-89870-982-7

ISBN 0-89870-982-2

Printed in Canada

*In Memory of the work
of the "Rosary Priest"
1909 – 1992*

Declaration

The decree of the Congregation for the Propagation of the Faith, A.A.S. 58, 1186 (approved by Pope Paul VI on 14 October 1966) states that the *Nihil Obstat* and *Imprimatur* are no longer required on publications that deal with private revelations, provided that they contain nothing contrary to faith or morals. The author wishes to manifest unconditional submission to the final and official judgment of the Magisterium of the Church in matters of faith and morals.

Contents

Preface

The Rosary is not merely a series of prayers to be recited; it is a series of thoughts to be dwelt on, to be turned over in the mind, to be applied in daily life. To say the Rosary well demands that it show results, that those who have prayed their beads get up from their knees and live different lives. For years I've hoped for a book on the Rosary that would be "practical" in the sense I've just described, but also beautiful. The beautiful Mother of God, the central figure in the Rosary, deserves the finest literary treatment accorded to any creature. We have penetrated into the recesses of heaven, it seems, to capture some of the sublime beauty of Mary, the Mother of God. But we have also been able, in a way that seems to me to be unequaled, to show the relevance of each mystery to today's work-a-day world. These thoughts, from the heart, are both lofty and down-to-earth. And I am happy to present them to all who love Mary and her Rosary. May all learn, through this exquisite little book, more of her and of her Divine Son.

Servant of God
Father Patrick Peyton, CSC
(1909 - 1992)

Foreword

Just as the origins and development of the Rosary consisted of an evolutionary process, this book, *Father Peyton's Rosary Prayer Book*, has also evolved through the years to the form in which we present it to you today.

When Father Patrick Peyton, CSC, began work on this book of reflections in 1951, his original thought was to put something small and compact into the hands of servicemen. Acting on the suggestion of U.S. Navy Chief of Chaplains Edward J. Hemphill, he wanted something that the servicemen as a group could use to guide or channel their prayers.

These reflections were created with the help of Father M. Charles Fiddler, OCSO, a Trappist monk of Spencer, Massachusetts, for what was known then as the Family Rosary Crusade. The texts of Scripture now come from the New American Bible.

Scripture tells us time and again that the most important thing is what is in our hearts. A person's heart is most revealed in their day-to-day actions.

It is in the gospel narratives that we come closest to understanding the true person of Jesus and Mary. It is in reflecting on humble and faithful incidents of the life of Jesus and Mary that we find a model of Christian living.

In our Holy Father's Apostolic Letter entitled, "Rosarium Virginis Mariae," dated October 16, 2002, Pope John Paul II stated, "The family that prays together stays together. The Holy Rosary, by age-old tradition, has shown itself particularly effective as a prayer which brings the family together. Individual family members, in turning their eyes towards Jesus, also regain the ability to look one another in the eye, to communicate, to show solidarity, to forgive one another and to see their covenant of love renewed in the Spirit of God."

Holy Cross Family Ministries embraces these Mysteries of Light and hopes that they will bring a deeper understanding for you of the Lord's public life. Keeping true to Father Peyton's reflections, we have decided to add the reflections on the Mysteries of Light in the same style as the original reflections.

It is our hope that through the use of this prayer

book two things will happen. First, may you be confirmed in the fact that you are already on the road to Christian living; and second, may you be further challenged to action through the example of the Mother of Jesus.

To those who already pray the Rosary with strong faith and devotion, I offer this invitation: Please reflect on the commentaries as a way of slowing down and savoring the various mysteries of the Rosary which tell so well the story of our redemption as a people of God, a family of families.

To those for whom the Rosary is a new and different way to pray I say: Let this meditative way of praying the Rosary help you appreciate the depth of God's love for us all. May Mary, the handmaid of the Lord who kept so much in her heart, touch our hearts and help us all respond to God with a simple "yes" after her example.

In Jesus, Son of God and Son of Mary,

Fr. John Phalen csc

Father John Phalen, CSC
President, Holy Cross Family Ministries

The Story of Father Peyton and Family Rosary

The life and work of Servant of God Father Patrick Peyton, CSC, reached millions. He shared and preached his incredible love, affection, and devotion to our God and Mary, holding out a promise of peace and blessing through family prayer, especially the Rosary.

Father Peyton was born on January 9, 1909, the sixth of nine children in the rural town of Carracastle located on the western coast of County Mayo, Ireland. He immigrated to the United States in 1928.

While working in the cathedral in Scranton, Pennsylvania, he heard the call of God to the priesthood and entered the seminary of the Congregation of Holy Cross at Notre Dame, Indiana. While he was in the seminary, he was diagnosed with advanced tuberculosis and little hope was given for his recovery. Father began to pray to God through the intercession of Mary. He was cured.

Newly ordained and burning with determination to spend his life in the service of our Blessed

Mother, Father Peyton knew exactly what to do. In gratitude to Mary for his remarkable recovery, he would devote his life and priesthood to proclaiming the value and necessity of family prayer, especially the daily family Rosary. He knew its value for as a child the family Rosary filled his family's home and hearts each day with the most challenging words that one can speak: "I believe in God" . . . "Our Father" . . . "Holy Mary, Mother of God, pray for us."

In 1942 he shared this message of love with churches, schools, and religious institutions in the United States. So great was the response and enthusiasm for the appeal that the effects were soon felt on three other continents. Recognizing the need for the message to be heard by all, Father Peyton turned to the power of mass media.

In 1947 Father Peyton's Family Theater made its debut on radio. He engaged listeners by offering stories that taught moral values. Leading Hollywood figures recognized the importance of this work and wanted to be a part of it.

In 1948 Father Peyton initiated the first of many

worldwide crusades. Millions of people gathered to hear him speak on many occasions. His conviction in the power of prayer and his love for Mary emanated from him as he spoke.

In 1957 Father Peyton completed the production of 15 films that depicted the Mysteries of the Rosary. They are still airing today all over the world.

Father Peyton carried his message to over 28 million people through personal addresses, the written word, radio, film and television. His slogans – *The family that prays together stays together* and *A world at prayer is a world at peace* – captivated audiences worldwide. Four popes recognized and approved this great man's efforts to promote the unity and sanctity of the family. Father Peyton's life work became *his magnificat* to Mary. Father Peyton died on June 3, 1992, in San Pedro, California. In his final moments his words were "Mary, my Queen, my Mother."

On June 1, 2001, Bishop Sean O'Malley of the Diocese of Fall River, Massachusetts, USA, announced that he had received notification from the Vatican's Congregation for the Causes of Saints that the cause for sainthood for Father Patrick Peyton, CSC, can proceed. Father Peyton is buried in Easton, Massachusetts, which is within the Diocese of Fall River.

The ministry of Father Peyton continues today under the direction of the Congregation of Holy Cross. Family Rosary is a member of Holy Cross Family Ministries which is comprised of Family Rosary, FamilyTheater Productions, Father Peyton Family Institute and Family Rosary International. Each ministers to families in diverse but complementary ways. Family Rosary thrives in more than a dozen countries on five continents, making our message of prayer and family unity global.

History of the Rosary

The Rosary has been a major influence in Roman Catholic thought for over 500 years while paving the way for a greater understanding of the mystery of Christ celebrated within family prayer. It stands as the tradition-distilled essence of Christian devotion in which vocal and mental prayer unite the whole person in effective and purposeful meditation on the central mysteries of Christian belief. The Rosary thus joins the human race to God through Mary whom God chose from all time for the specific purposes of mother and intercessor.

The historical development of the Rosary begins with the desert fathers and their need to find a system to ease their laborious and repetitive prayer life. It is generally agreed by scholars that a system for counting repetitive prayers began with the Hindus some nine centuries before Christ. In the Christian era, desert monks used rocks, sticks or notches in wood to count the prayers they recited. Over time, prayer, generally the psalms, was united into a "three groups of fifty" format (*Na tri coicat*) so that "fifties" could be used for personal and/or penitential prayer. By the twelfth century it was common for all Christians to carry a "*Paternoster cord*" on their person for purposes of keeping straight the prayers recited on any group of fifty.

As the need for lay participation in the prayer life of the Church increased, the need for a Psalter of popular prayers (most people of the period were not sufficiently educated to pray the psalms in Latin) became urgent. Thus the *Na tri coicat* format was imposed first on recitations of *Paternosters* and later on *Aves*. Spurred by the association of Mary with roses and rose gardens, from both scriptural and traditional bases, the Marian Psalter of *Aves* became by the fourteenth century a standard form of repetitive prayer for the whole Church, laity and religious alike.

The fifteenth century provided the development period for the many facets of today's Rosary. During this period the Dominican influence with the Rosary grew and was fostered through both fact and legend. Although many apocryphal accounts exist to explain how St. Dominic and his followers became originators of Rosary devotion, it is evident that these accounts cannot stand up to the scrutiny of historical research. Although the Dominicans were not the sole originators of the Rosary, their influence on the growth, devotion and spread of this prayer was significant. It would not be inaccurate to call them the principal promoters and defenders of the Rosary through history. Certainly the fifteenth century was a period for much Dominican influence in this meditation, bringing a series of prayers and mysteries into a coherent form of prayer.

The fifteenth century saw the Rosary begin its development into the familiar prayer form we know today. The Our Father came intact from the Gospel of Matthew. The Hail Mary developed from the scriptural greetings of Gabriel and Elizabeth to Mary in Luke's Gospel, plus a popular exhortation in use by the laity of that period. The Glory Be was used as a common doxology from the earliest of Christian times when praying the psalms. The *Salve Regina*, a later addition to the Rosary, states all relevant medieval themes about the Blessed Virgin Mary. Its affiliation with the Rosary came about through popular practice, although its precise origin within the devotion is not known. The Apostles' Creed along with the Rosary pendant were also later developments, being added to the Rosary only in the early seventeenth century. During this period the definition of the individual prayers, plus the development of a series of mysteries which united this loosely connected series of prayers, took place. The mysteries, the true essence of the Rosary, have their origin from Henry of Kalbar who added *clausulae* or "statements of faith" to each of the fifty *Aves* of the Marian Psalter. The development of the mysteries included the fixing of 150 statements of faith which were followed by the introduction of fifteen true mysteries, one for each *Paternoster*. Eventually the *clausulae* faded away and the fifteen mysteries remained. By the mid-sixteenth century, the mysteries we know today, joyful, sorrowful, and glorious, were in place and used in Rosary recitation.

The most significant event in the historical derivation of the Rosary was the formation of the Rosary confraternity in 1470 by Blessed Alanus de Rupe. The communal attitude (praying in groups) that the Confraternity promoted raised the whole consciousness of the Christian world to the Rosary. The second half of the sixteenth century saw the Confraternity's work rewarded with the Church's official recognition of the Rosary. On October 7, 1571, Pope St. Pius V declared that because of the assistance of the Rosary in securing victory over the Turks at Lepanto, a commemoration in honor of the Rosary would henceforth be held on that date. Two years later the Feast of the Most Holy Rosary was established by Pope Gregory XIII;

the date is still celebrated in our contemporary liturgical calendar.

The work of Pope Leo XIII in promotion of the Rosary is a landmark in the evolving history of this most glorious prayer of devotion to Mary. More than any other pontiff, Leo wrote extensively on the Rosary, completing twelve encyclicals and numerous other letters, apostolic exhortations and similar works. In his twenty-five year pontificate Leo touched on all aspects of the Rosary devotion. All of his teachings, however, were centered about the concept that by using the Rosary, one could most efficaciously reach Mary, and through her intercession, her son Jesus Christ. Pope Leo wanted to restore the Rosary to a prominent position within the devotional life of the Church. His work was most certainly successful, as evidenced by the great popularity of the Rosary during the first half of the twentieth century.

The voices of those who have promoted the Rosary have continued to speak. Probably the most significant comment which has come forward is the emphasis on the family as the principal body around which the Rosary can be most effectively utilized. Pope Pius XII spoke of the efficacious use of the Rosary in the family setting. The Pope's words were in keeping with the trend initiated in 1942 by Father Patrick Peyton, CSC, who became internationally known as "The Rosary Priest." Through his Family Theater Productions and international Rosary crusades, the Rosary and family prayer became common practices in the typical Roman Catholic household. Father Peyton's slogan, "The family that prays together stays together," became a rallying cry for many of the faithful.

Popes John XXIII and Paul VI introduced new teachings on the Rosary while continuing the teachings of their predecessors. For Pope John, the Rosary was the universal prayer for all the redeemed. Additionally, he taught that the Mysteries of the Rosary must have a three-fold purpose: mystical contemplation, intimate reflection, and pious intention. Pope Paul also emphasized the importance of the mysteries, saying that the prayers of the Rosary were merely an empty shell without the mysteries. Both popes continued to foster the family Rosary through writings and support of Father Peyton's Rosary crusade. The views of the pontiffs show that Rosary recitation and teaching continues to be important in our contemporary prayer devotion.

The story of the Rosary cannot end without reference to the visions at Fatima and Mary's powerful message to pray the Rosary daily. In coming to Fatima with a message of prayer and peace, the Blessed Virgin Mary, through the visions of October 13, 1917, has herself given to the world the true value of the Rosary. The world came to know that with the Rosary it had a weapon which could bring peace to our troubled society then and remain a powerful tool in the ever-present battle to maintain peace in our present-day, very difficult and complex world.

Father Richard Gribble, CSC

How to Pray the Rosary

The Rosary is a prayer of meditation. We use the beads to focus our attention on the life of Christ through the Joyful, Sorrowful and Glorious Mysteries.

Praying in this way helps us to link our lives with what we know of the life of Jesus, Mary and Joseph. It is one way God can show us that there is no part of our joy, pain or glory where He is not present.

There are two common ways to pray the Rosary in use today. One gathers all the prayers together to be said at once. This can be done alone or with a group (as in a family Rosary). The second method allows us to take a whole day to pray.

The Rosary is a way to meditate on the life of Christ. Each group of 10 beads is called a decade. Before each decade recall the part of the life of Jesus it represents.

1. Make the sign of the cross and pray the Apostles' Creed
2. Pray the Our Father
3. Pray 3 Hail Marys and the Glory Be
4. Announce the 1st Mystery, pray the Our Father
5. Pray 10 Hail Marys and end with Glory Be
6. Announce the 2nd Mystery, pray the Our Father
7. Pray 10 Hail Marys and end with Glory Be
8. Announce the 3rd Mystery, pray the Our Father
9. Pray 10 Hail Marys and end with Glory Be
10. Announce the 4th Mystery, pray the Our Father
11. Pray 10 Hail Marys and end with Glory Be
12. Announce the 5th Mystery, pray the Our Father
13. Pray 10 Hail Marys and end with Glory Be
14. Pray the Hail Holy Queen
15. Follow your local customs for other prayers at this point
16. Make the sign of the cross

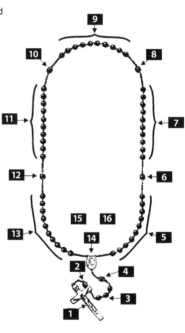

Method 1

1. Looking at the cross, we hold it while we make the sign of the cross and pray the Apostles' Creed which is a summary of all the things we believe as Catholics.

2. On this first large bead, we pray an Our Father, the prayer that Jesus taught us.

3. On each of the three smaller beads, we pray the Hail Mary. Then we pray the Glory Be.

4. On this next large bead, we announce the first mystery (eg. Joy, Light, Sorrow, Glory). We reflect on what happened to Jesus at this time and we think about what it means in our lives today. We pray the Our Father.

5. We pray one Hail Mary on each of the next ten beads. Then we pray the Glory Be.

6. On this large bead, we announce the next mystery, reflect, and pray the Our Father.

7. We pray one Hail Mary on each of the next ten beads. Then we pray the Glory Be.

8. At this large bead, we announce the next mystery, reflect, and pray the Our Father.

9. We pray one Hail Mary on each of the next ten beads. Then we pray the Glory Be.

10. On this large bead, we announce the next mystery, reflect, and pray the Our Father.

11. We pray one Hail Mary on each of the next ten beads. Then we pray the Glory Be.

12. On this large bead, we announce the next mystery, reflect, and pray the Our Father.

13. We pray one Hail Mary on each of the next ten beads. Then we pray the Glory Be.

14. We have now reached the end of the Rosary. On the medal that connects the beads we pray the Hail Holy Queen.

15. Please follow your local custom for other prayers at this point.

16. Make the sign of the cross.

Method 2

Meditating with the Rosary throughout the day
The Rosary tells the story of Jesus, how He came to be born, how He lived, how He died and how He rose. It helps us call to mind the relationship Jesus had with His Mother Mary.

We picture these events or 'mysteries,' which occurred in the life of Jesus and spend time placing ourselves in the picture we imagine. This helps us connect with the action of God in the event and in our lives today.

In the first Joyful Mystery an angel announces to Mary that God is with her and has a very special role for her to play. She is asked to accept and she says "yes." We imagine what it was like for this teenage girl to say yes to being the Mother of Jesus. We then focus our attention on the ways God is calling us to say yes. We ask for Mary's help as we recite the ten Hail Marys.

During the day as we travel to work or school or go about our morning tasks, we continue to meditate as we remember Mary's trip to visit her cousin Elizabeth. We reflect on the way Mary and

Elizabeth experienced God's presence during this visit. We then focus on the many ways God visits us during the day. We ask Mary to help us recognize God in all we do as we pray the ten Hail Marys.

We continue this process with all five events in the Joyful Mysteries. By the end of the day we have reached the last decade of the Joyful Mysteries. We reflect on the joy and confusion felt by Mary and Joseph in the temple where they found Jesus. Where did you find Jesus today? Was it in a poor person on the street, an elderly neighbor, a friend, a child, or your husband or wife?

Praying this way throughout the day helps us keep God as the center of our lives. It helps prayer become more than a moment or two with God – it becomes a way of life!

Prayers of the Rosary

The Apostles' Creed is a summary of what we believe as Catholic Christians.

The Apostles' Creed: *I believe in God, the Father almighty, creator of heaven and earth. I believe in Jesus Christ, his only Son, our Lord. He was conceived by the power of the Holy Spirit and born of the Virgin Mary. He suffered under Pontius Pilate, was crucified, died and was buried. He descended to the dead. On the third day He rose again. He ascended into heaven and is seated at the right hand of the Father. He will come again to judge the living and the dead. I believe in the Holy Spirit, the holy Catholic Church, the communion of saints, the forgiveness of sins, the resurrection of the body, and the life everlasting. Amen.*

The large single beads are used to count the Our Fathers – this is the prayer that Jesus taught His disciples when they asked Him how to pray.

Our Father: *Our Father, Who art in Heaven, Hallowed be Thy Name. Thy Kingdom come. Thy Will be done, on earth as it is in Heaven. Give us this day our daily bread. And forgive us our trespasses, as we forgive those who trespass against us. And lead us not into temptation, but deliver us from evil. Amen.*

The smaller beads are used to count the Hail Marys – the prayer that recounts the angel's greeting and what Elizabeth had to say to Mary while she was pregnant with Jesus.

Hail Mary: *Hail Mary, full of grace, the Lord is with you. Blessed are you among women and blessed is the fruit of your womb, Jesus. Holy Mary,*

Mother of God, pray for us sinners, now and at the hour of our death. Amen.

The medal which connects the bead is used by some to say the Hail Holy Queen – or Salve Regina, which was a hymn widely used in church services during the middle ages. By the 17th century it was part of the Rosary although little is known of how that came to be.

Hail Holy Queen: *Hail Holy Queen, Mother of Mercy, our life, our sweetness, and our hope. To you do we cry poor banished children of Eve. To you do we send up our sighs, mourning and weeping in this valley of tears. Turn then, O most gracious advocate, your eyes of mercy toward us and after this our exile, show unto us the blessed fruit of your womb, Jesus. O clement! O loving! O sweet Virgin Mary! Pray for us, O Holy Mother of God. That we may be made worthy of the promises of Christ.*

Many people pray the doxology after the ten Hail Marys. The doxology: "Glory be to the Father, to the Son and to the Holy Spirit," is based on an ancient Jewish prayer. The prayer has been used by many in their family recitation of the Rosary.

Glory Be: *Glory be to the Father, and to the Son, and to the Holy Spirit. As it was in the beginning, is now, and ever shall be, world without end. Amen.*

The Joyful Mysteries

The Mysteries and Their Scriptural References

(Traditionally said on Mondays and Thursdays. These may be said on Mondays and Saturdays if the Mysteries of Light are used on Thursdays.)

1) The Annunciation (Luke 1:26-28)

2) The Visitation (Luke 1:39-45)

3) The Birth of Our Lord (Luke 2:1-20)

4) The Presentation in the Temple (Luke 2:22-35)

5) The Finding of the Child Jesus in the Temple (Luke 2:41-52)

The Sorrowful Mysteries

(To be said on Tuesdays and Fridays)

1) The Agony in the Garden (Matthew 26:36-46)

2) The Scourging at the Pillar (Mark 15:1-16)

3) The Crowning with Thorns (Matthew 27:27-31)

4) The Carrying of the Cross (Mark 15:20-22)

5) The Crucifixion (Luke 23:33-46)

The Glorious Mysteries

Traditionally said on Wednesdays and Saturdays and some Sundays. If the Mysteries of Light are used, the Glorious Mysteries may be said on Wednesdays and Sundays.)

1) The Resurrection (Matthew 28:1-10)

2) The Ascension of Our Lord (Luke 24:44-53)

3) The Descent of the Holy Spirit (John 14:15-21)

4) The Assumption of Our Lady into Heaven★

5) The Coronation of the Blessed Virgin Mary★

★ There are no exact scriptural references. Please check Catholic Catechism, paragraph 966.

(Note: On Saturdays and Sundays during Advent and Lent, the Joyful Mysteries and Sorrowful Mysteries respectively, are used. On Thursdays, the Mysteries of Light may be prayed.)

30

The Meditations

The Joyful Mysteries

The Annunciation
The Visitation
The Birth of our Lord
The Presentation in the
  Temple
The Finding of the Child
  Jesus in the Temple

LOVING GOD

Our Lady will give us a deeper understanding of
our privilege of *loving God* through the five Joyful
Mysteries

—one—
Our Father, Who art in Heaven...
—ten—
Hail Mary, full of grace...
—one—
Glory be to the Father...

I. THE ANNUNCIATION

"Mary, do not be afraid; you have found favor with God."   *Luke 1:30*

ANOTHER day had begun in the little home of Nazareth – a quiet, cool March day. Mary would spend it as she had spent countless others, working about the house. A young teenage girl, Mary, ordinary like the rest of the villagers, like Joseph ...Suddenly, an angel was by her side: "Hail, full of grace!" An ordinary person would be rather disturbed by such a visitor, and by such a greeting. And Mary was! "She was troubled at his word." The angel had implied that Mary loved God with all her heart, soul, mind, strength; and she did.

Loving God wholeheartedly – like Mary, I was created to do just that – and being "ordinary" puts no barriers in my way!

II. THE VISITATION

"During those days Mary set out and traveled to the hill country in haste...to the house of Zechariah and greeted Elizabeth."   *Luke 1:39*

MARY was a model human being, unselfish, heart full of affection. Jesus was now divinely conceived in her womb. We might want to stay home and love Him, love Him alone. But Mary knew this was not the way to love God: to love God alone is to love Him not at all. Of her Son's commandment, "Love one another," Mary's visitation was an unconscious prophecy. Loving God requires that I love everyone else – even those I cannot like! How do I do that? Practice seeing Christ in others, and act accordingly. "What you do for others, you do to me." Christ meant that.

III. THE BIRTH OF OUR LORD

"You will find an infant wrapped in swaddling clothes and lying in a manger." Luke 2:12

MARY and Joseph found accommodations in one of Bethlehem's hillside caves. It offered some protection from the December night, nothing more. Air, heavy with moisture seeping through damp earthen walls; stifling odors of cattle; darkness made all the more emphatic by a lantern's frail light and the smallest patch of night horizon, too low for stars – yes, there would be room here. And here, Mary and Joseph loved God and God loved Mary, Joseph and God's Son, Jesus.

God can be loved – wholeheartedly – anywhere. Loving God does not depend on the kind of place I'm in – it depends on the kind of person I am.

IV. THE PRESENTATION IN THE TEMPLE

"My soul proclaims the greatness of the Lord; my spirit rejoices in God my savior."   Luke 1:46

WE think of Mary as a reflective woman. Her recorded words are few; when others speak, she "ponders their words in her heart." Mary spent her life in the far corners of her soul. She spent her life being all God wanted her to be. When she does speak, Mary sings. A lark in the light of morning never sang so sweetly. "My soul magnifies the Lord!...rejoices in God!...Who is mighty, Holy is God's name!" Mary's love flowed out of her.

Loving God makes a heart that sings.

V. THE FINDING OF THE CHILD JESUS IN THE TEMPLE

"After three days, they found him in the Temple."
Luke 2:46

IN three syllables, this Mystery of the Rosary reveals the very root and fibre of love for God; it tells exactly what loving God means. "They found him." A perfect expression of our meditation's theme. To love God is nothing else than to have found Jesus. The explanation is no less simply told: all my love for God is from Christ; the outpouring of grace upon the world is His meriting. Every spark of divine charity, the briefest and brightest in every soul in every age, has been struck to life on one Cornerstone – Christ.

Mary's Son came into the world to look for me that I might find the Father. I find Jesus and the Father in the Sacraments, the Mass, in my neighbor. Am I watching for Jesus, wholeheartedly, as Mary was?

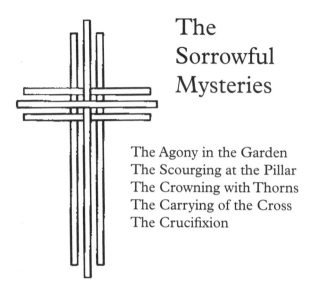

The Sorrowful Mysteries

The Agony in the Garden
The Scourging at the Pillar
The Crowning with Thorns
The Carrying of the Cross
The Crucifixion

SUFFERING

Our Lady will give us a deeper understanding of *suffering* through the five Sorrowful Mysteries

—one—
Our Father, Who art in Heaven...
—ten—
Hail Mary, full of grace...
—one—
Glory be to the Father...

I. THE AGONY IN THE GARDEN

"Father, if you are willing take this cup away from me; still, not my will but yours be done."

Luke 22:42

CHRIST knew He would suffer. He spent His life speaking the truth. Those in authority did not like Him. Mary carried many fears for her Son in her heart. John hailed Him as the meek Lamb of God. Jesus spoke often of His death; invited others to do what He was about to do – "take up the Cross;" then deliberately went up to Jerusalem to His earthly doom. But when that long-awaited suffering was only a sunrise away, Jesus Christ fell upon His Face and bled at the thought of pain and asked that, if it were possible, the chalice be withheld.

To tremble at pain is Christlike. Suffering is not a good thing that merely appears evil. It is an evil which human nature shrinks from – and grace can sanctify.

II. THE SCOURGING AT THE PILLAR

"I shall have him flogged."   *Luke 23:16*

CHRIST shrank from pain, but did not refuse it. Late morning saw Jesus flung against a praetorium pillar, while the hired men of Rome wore themselves out whipping and lashing Him near to death. Every thump of the iron-weighted cords tore fresh red rents in His Flesh. Jesus, who the night before had turned wine into Blood, now shed that Blood like wine poured out. His Body is the chalice of His spilt-out Blood, and the cup He no longer asks His Father to remove.

God knows how desperate we feel when we ask Him to relieve our sufferings because God was with Jesus in all Jesus' pain. To accept pain as Jesus did is to sanctify it – and myself.

III. THE CROWNING WITH THORNS

"And the soldiers wove a crown out of thorns and placed it on his head."   *John 19:2*

JESUS has been officially sentenced to death. However, the soldiers were in no hurry to finish off their prey. To the twisted wits of the soldiers, the praetorium courtyard suggested a mock court, and Jesus a mock King. Injury was added to insult when they clamped the King's head in a royal crown, studded with thorns.

Jesus, the innocence of God, had no safeguard against pain.

IV. THE CARRYING OF THE CROSS

"Simon, a Cyrenian, carried the cross behind Jesus."
Luke 23:26

BY God's command, the Mosaic Law summoned every Jewish man to the Holy City for the Passover. Simon, from faraway Cyrene, was only one poor, tired rustic among the hundreds of thousands of pilgrims dutifully thronging to Jerusalem. By chance he crossed the path of the soldiers leading Jesus to Calvary; by chance, Jesus fell to His knees just then; by chance, the guards caught sight of Simon and bullied him into service. Simon was taking part in the solemn ritual for which he had come – the sacrifice of the Paschal Lamb.

It is characteristic of the cross that it comes to us "by chance." Remember, when we suffer, Jesus is with us in our pain helping us carry our cross.

V. THE CRUCIFIXION

"One of them ran to get a sponge; he soaked it in wine; and putting it on a reed, gave it to him to drink."   *Matthew 27:48*

THE bite of the whip kept Jesus conscious until He reached Calvary. There two soldiers tore away His clothing, which the drying blood had glued to His lashed Body. The morning's endless scourging was relived in a single moment. Jesus reeled from the sudden torture. A coarse narcotic of wine, myrrh, and incense was put quickly to His lips – not to relieve His thirst, but to numb His senses. Jesus did not take the drug.

The gate of heaven has a cross for a key. It is Jesus who forged the key.

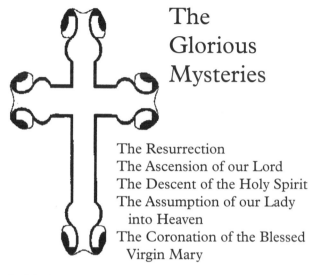

The Glorious Mysteries

The Resurrection
The Ascension of our Lord
The Descent of the Holy Spirit
The Assumption of our Lady
   into Heaven
The Coronation of the Blessed
   Virgin Mary

HOPE

Our Lady will give us a deeper understanding of
hope through the five Glorious Mysteries

> —one—
> Our Father, Who art in Heaven...
> —ten—
> Hail Mary, full of grace...
> —one—
> Glory be to the Father...

I. THE RESURRECTION

"They have taken the Lord from the tomb, and we don't know where they put him." John 20:2

THE Gospel of John tells us that just before Jesus made His last journey to Jerusalem, He gathered His disciples about Him and said plainly: "The Son of Man is to be abandoned into the hands of men. They are going to kill Him. Three days later He will rise again." These last words which strike such a triumphant note were not understood by the disciples. "They were overcome with sorrow." Their bitter grief proved their great love for Jesus, but it also proved their utter lack of hope in His glorious Easter victory over sin and death.

Christ's Resurrection was not just a marvelous event. It drove despair out of the world. It was Christ's way of promising that we too shall live forever.

II. THE ASCENSION OF OUR LORD

"The Lord Jesus was taken up into heaven... they went forth and preached everywhere."

Mark 16:19-20

WHEN Jesus returned to His friends on Easter day, some were too incredulous, others too broken-hearted, to recognize Him. Mary Magdalen, her sight blurred by tears, thought He was the gardener. Two disciples, meeting Him on the road to Emmaus, took Him for a stranger. When He appeared to the Apostles, they were terrified – "A ghost!" Yet on the day of His Ascension, when He left them, His disciples were filled with joy! They were beginning to understand God's way of doing things and even Christ's departure didn't dampen their hopes for the future.

Jesus told His disciples that He must leave them so the Spirit could come. In times of trouble, remember we are not alone, the Spirit of God is with us.

III. THE DESCENT OF THE HOLY SPIRIT

"And it happened that while they were conversing...
Jesus drew near and walked with them."

Luke 24:15

ON Easter day Jesus met two of His disciples
near Emmaus. They did not recognize Him; so
(perhaps with a twinkle in His eye) He asked,
"What makes you so gloomy?" At once they
poured out the whole heartbreaking story of
their shattered hopes. "We had hoped that it was
Jesus who would deliver Israel; but now..." and
they shook their heads. Easter was a day of sorrow for the Apostles. Pentecost was quite another
day. Then Jesus, having ascended to heaven, sent
the Holy Spirit upon His disciples in the form of
tongues of fire. Immediately they went forth to
preach Jesus Christ – with fiery tongues.

The Apostles, convinced of their own hopeless-
ness, learned from the Holy Spirit to hope in
Christ. Humility is the mother of perfect hope.

IV. THE ASSUMPTION OF OUR LADY INTO HEAVEN

"Mary, preserved free from all stains of original sin, when the source of her earthly life was finished, was taken up body and soul into heavenly glory."

Pius XII Munificentissimus Deus (1950)

FROM the moment of His conception in Mary's womb, Jesus knew His Father. He would live a very down-to-earth life, and would need the hope that only God can offer. *Mary's* hope, then, is a most perfect share in the hope of Jesus.

The Church calls Mary the Mother of Sacred Hope. She is the most exalted model of perfect confidence in God. Hail Holy Queen, our life, our sweetness, and our hope! After this, our exile, show unto us the blessed Fruit of your womb, Jesus.

V. THE CORONATION OF THE BLESSED VIRGIN MARY

"There, 'in the glory of the Most Holy and Undivided Trinity,' in the communion of all the saints, the Church is awaited by the one she venerates as Mother of her Lord and as her own mother."

Catechism, no. 972

AT her Immaculate Conception, Mary's soul was endowed with an intense degree of Hope; but the full perfection of that Hope was crowned in heaven only after a lifetime of trials. Her Hope, like all her virtues and perfections, centered around her trust in God. Jesus was the object of her Faith – her Baby, her Boy, her Son. Jesus was the object of her Love. God was the object of her perfect Hope. As she stood near Jesus on Calvary – He with a lance in His side, she with a sword in her soul – only her boundless trust in God kept her from dying of sorrow.

While there's hope, there's life. Mary was hopeful, even on Calvary, because she saw God's will in everything. Hopefulness is a virtue God expects of me.

51

Personal Notes

52

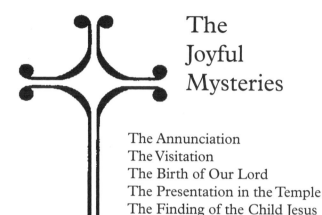

The Joyful Mysteries

The Annunciation
The Visitation
The Birth of Our Lord
The Presentation in the Temple
The Finding of the Child Jesus
    in the Temple

WHAT GOD EXPECTS OF ME

Our Lady will give us a deeper understanding of *what God expects of me* through the five Joyful Mysteries

—one—
Our Father, Who art in Heaven...
—ten—
Hail Mary, full of grace...
—one—
Glory be to the Father...

53

I. THE ANNUNCIATION

"Behold, you will conceive in your womb and bear a son, and you shall name him Jesus."

Luke 1:31

TWO thousand years ago the human race made sinful choices. Rome's chief commerce was vice. People were left to their own desires; God appeared to be forgotten – except in the little home at Nazareth. God was certainly there, hidden in the Virgin Mary's womb, as if He had to steal into His own world. A young girl's "Yes," let God do what God wanted to do in her life.

We still make sinful choices. God seems to be only here and there; sin and selfishness everywhere in between. What can I do? What Mary did – say yes. Obey God's laws of love; live up to the duties of my state in life. The world needs my day-by-day "Fiat." Mary is a model of what God expects of me.

II. THE VISITATION

*"Elizabeth...in her old age, has also conceived a son,
and this is the sixth month for her who was called
barren."*   *Luke 1:36*

WASN'T this just like Mary, to be perceptive.
"Elizabeth has conceived a son"; an angel drops
a hint! Not a single word of command, not even
a "Would you mind...?" Just a simple statement
of fact. By divine design – "nothing is impossible
with God" – Mary's aged cousin is already six
months with child. Mary's heart listened between
the lines. She "took the hint." A grateful Elizabeth
could rest until her time would come, while "the
Mother of her Lord" did the housekeeping.

When I "lend a hand" without being asked,
without needing to be asked, I am like Mary.
"Fiat" again "Be it done" by me!

III. THE BIRTH OF OUR LORD

"A decree went out from Caesar Augustus that the whole world should be enrolled."   Luke 2:1

FOR nearly nine months Mary had borne Jesus in her womb; her time was now at hand. She would like to think only of Him. Joseph left her to her quiet meditation, but Caesar did not. In obedience to the emperor's ambition, she had to travel the wearying hills to Bethlehem where a cave was her Son's first home.

Sad? Unfortunate? Hard to take? Not for Mary. She went where Caesar commanded her to go, as willingly as she had obeyed the angel Gabriel, and for the same reason – she saw in both God's will for her. A "Fiat" that is all mine!

IV. THE PRESENTATION IN THE TEMPLE

"Every male that opens the womb shall be consecrated to the Lord."   *Luke 2:23*

MARY'S heart is alive with thanksgiving as she carries her Child into His Father's house "according to the custom of the law." Until the Church of her Son, the Church whose Mother she is, had blossomed forth from Judaism, Mary would do as God had prescribed "through the law and the prophets."

Jesus came to teach us about the love of God. The Holy Spirit helps us to be God's Church and live that law of love. Through the sacraments and daily prayer, we become stronger and more able to love.

V. THE FINDING OF THE CHILD JESUS IN THE TEMPLE

"Each year His parents went to Jerusalem for the feast of Passover and when he was twelve years old, they went up according to festival custom."

Luke 2:41-42

JOSEPH, like Mary, had complied with angels' commands and an emperor's decree. Now in obedience to the law, he has journeyed to Jerusalem to celebrate the Passover with Mary and the boy Jesus. Unknown to His parents, Jesus remained behind as they left by caravan for Nazareth. After three days of agonizing search, Mary and Joseph found Him in the Temple, obediently "about His Father's business."

Jesus, Mary, Joseph, in your lives there were many unknowns. You had to trust so often. You had faith in God's messengers, willingness to obey civil laws, and hope that one day you would understand what "My Father's business" was. Help me to have that faith and hope.

The Sorrowful Mysteries

The Agony in the Garden
The Scourging at the Pillar
The Crowning with Thorns
The Carrying of the Cross
The Crucifixion

THE CRUCIFIXION

Our Lady will give us a deeper understanding of
the *crucifixion* through the five Sorrowful Mysteries

—one—
Our Father, Who art in Heaven...
—ten—
Hail Mary, full of grace...
—one—
Glory be to the Father...

I. THE AGONY IN THE GARDEN

"Then going out He went, as was His custom, to the Mount of Olives, and the disciples followed Him."
Luke 22:39

DURING Jesus' public life, He often took the road less traveled and did the unexpected. Jesus had multiplied five barley loaves into a banquet for thousands. When His grateful guests called Him their Christ and their king, Jesus slipped away to a mountain alone. In Mark's gospel, the crowds exulted and children sang as Jesus rode on an ass into Jerusalem. But even though the stones were ready to break out in Hosannas, Jesus would not be a king. Yet in Gethsemane, at the mercy of those with murder in their hearts, Jesus is content to let the crowd have its way with Him.

Deliberately, Jesus tried to show His followers that success in this life was not His goal. He never gained material things as a result of doing God's will.

II. THE SCOURGING AT THE PILLAR

"Again Pilate addressed them, still wishing to release Jesus, but they continued their shouting."

Luke 23:20

JESUS had come to preach to Israel's lost sheep, but His good news was for the Gentiles as well. And from the beginning, their lives touched. The prophet Isaiah tells us "a shoot shall sprout from the stump of Jesse." King Herod directed pagan Magi to His birthplace. Exiled from Jewish Palestine, the Christ Child hallowed Egypt by His hidden presence. Jesus found no faith in Israel like the ready trust of a Roman centurion; and while His brethren sought to kill Him, a Gentile woman begged His mercy. But in Christ's Passion, Pilate, with a coward's strange logic, declared, "I find no fault in Him, therefore will I scourge Him."

Jesus was a failure in everybody's eyes, except His Father's. Jesus wanted only to be true to what God the Father expected of Him. Whom do I choose to impress by my actions?

III. THE CROWNING WITH THORNS

"Pilate handed Jesus over to them to deal with as they wished."   *Luke 23:25*

JESUS knew the end was near. The road had been long and filled with disappointments. Remember how He was received in His hometown. "Impudent son of Joseph!" He continuously warned His disciples to beware and to expect the same fate that awaited Him. He even said, "Woe upon you, when men speak well of you!" It was too much for this world that God should walk among us. Sceptered, robed and crowned, the captive King of the Jews sat enthroned on the praetorium pavement while the cohort bowed low before Him and spat at His face.

My days are also filled with disappointments. But I am not alone. Jesus stands with me as others mock me.

IV. THE CARRYING OF THE CROSS

"They pressed into service a passerby Simon,
a Cyrenian."   Mark 15:21

WERE his opponents pleased by the sight of this
tortured man? Surely the Pharisees must have
recalled the day when Jesus proclaimed His great
challenge: "Will you be on My side? Then take up
the cross and follow after Me." And now, "This
man who lays a heavy burden on other men's
backs" – the Pharisees, often accused of this crime
by Jesus, must have taunted Him with His own
words as Simon seized the heavy cross – "and will
not lift a finger to carry it Himself!"

How we can turn words around and make them
mean what was never intended? Jesus help me
curb my tongue.

V. THE CRUCIFIXION

"At noon darkness came over the whole land until three in the afternoon." Mark 15:33

AS the world judges, Jesus was defeated. Betrayed and deserted by His friends; declared a criminal and crucified with two revolutionaries. His miraculous powers hushed, His good name gone, even His clothing snatched away; thrown against the cross while Pharisees made crude remarks about nailing the carpenter to His wood; hoisted up for all to laugh at; giving His Mother away; then feeling abandoned by His Father; and while the black fires of hell overshadowed Him, Jesus Christ died.

When the trials of my life cause me to feel abandoned by those who love me and by God, help me to remember Jesus is always with me.

The Glorious Mysteries

The Resurrection
The Ascension of our Lord
The Descent of the Holy Spirit
The Assumption of our Lady
into Heaven
The Coronation of the Blessed
Virgin Mary

SUCCESS

Our Lady will give us a deeper understanding of
success through the five Glorious Mysteries

—one—
Our Father, Who art in Heaven...
—ten—
Hail Mary, full of grace...
—one—
Glory be to the Father...

I. THE RESURRECTION

"They found the stone rolled away from the tomb; but when they entered, they did not find the body of the Lord Jesus."   *Luke 24:2-3*

JESUS had no need of earthly glory. His birth had been obscure, His parents ordinary folk. He worked as a carpenter for many years to support His widowed mother. Though His miracles made Him a public figure, on Calvary He spoke and acted only to reveal the Father's love. Jesus wanted us to know the Father in a new and definitive way. He felt no need to be an imposing person. He used ordinary images when He spoke: the farmer who planted grain, the woman who had lost a coin, the unjust judge who finally makes a decision because he can't take any more nagging.

And now the tomb is empty. How could this be? Did they not remember His words "and on the third day be raised?"

II. THE ASCENSION OF OUR LORD

"Why are you men from Galilee standing here looking into the sky?" Acts 1:11

THE Apostles stood on Olivet, eyes wide open, their gaze turned heavenward, their hearts beating hard. Jesus had just vanished from their sight above a silvery cloud that shimmered in the radiance of His glow. He had come to earth as a helpless Child; now He was leaving this earthly home as the world's Redeemer. The little group on Olivet stood in silent, joyful prayer, their hearts ascending with Him. Heaven was reflected in their eyes – until angels' chiding words brought them hurriedly down to earth.

Christ's cross was the road to His glorious Ascension. That is why the angels sent the Apostles back to the city – to take up their daily lives filled with joys and sorrows. A lesson for me!

III. THE DESCENT OF THE HOLY SPIRIT

"Hearing this, they were cut to the heart and said to Peter, 'what must we do?'"   *Acts 2:37*

ON Pentecost, the Church's birthday, three thousand candles were lit – three thousand souls enlightened with the grace of faith. From the simple eloquence of the Apostle Peter went forth the power of God, and those who had that morning been citizens of a dozen nations, and strangers to one another, were now "one in Christ." Their sudden, spontaneous confession that a crucified Nazarene was God and Savior was a stupendous miracle of God's grace, as well as a testimonial to our inviolable free will. The grace of Pentecost was offered to many, but it bore fruit only in those who opened their hearts to it.

Thank you God for the gift of faith. Help me to use my free will to grow in grace.

IV. THE ASSUMPTION OF OUR LADY INTO HEAVEN

"By her complete adherence to the Father's will, to his Son's redemptive work, and to every prompting of the Holy Spirit, the Virgin Mary is the Church's model of faith and charity."   Catechism, no. 967

AN echo, although it has a sound of its own, presupposes some other sound. So Mary's Assumption, in itself a glorious mystery, harks back to the still greater mystery of Christ's Incarnation. God came into the world by His own divine power. Mary, although the chosen one, was still but a creature, as little able to do anything without God's help as you and I. She was, then, glorified by the power of God. And as Calvary was the price of her Son's victory, so Mary's Assumption was preceded by her life of service.

Mary's triumph was like her Son's because her heart was like His. Real success is found only in thinking and acting like Christ.

69

V. THE CORONATION OF THE BLESSED VIRGIN MARY

"She is 'clearly the mother of the members of Christ'... since she has by her charity joined in bringing about the birth of believers in The Church..."

Catechism, no. 963

AT the Last Supper, Jesus gave the disciples two sacred rites to perform: to change bread and wine into His Body and Blood and to wash one another's feet. Mary was given the honor of bringing that Body and Blood into the world. She was given the task of helping the Church to continue to "Do this in memory" of her son. If we ask her, Mary will teach us how to wash each other's feet. She lived for others.

Mary was crowned Queen of Heaven only after a life of selfless service on earth. Mary teach me to serve others.

Personal Notes

72

The Joyful Mysteries

The Annunciation
The Visitation
The Birth of our Lord
The Presentation in the Temple
The Finding of the Child Jesus
   in the Temple

THE EUCHARIST

Our Lady will give us a deeper understanding of
the *Eucharist* through the five Joyful Mysteries

—one—
Our Father, Who art in Heaven...
—ten—
Hail Mary, full of grace...
—one—
Glory be to the Father...

I. THE ANNUNCIATION

*"The angel Gabriel was sent from God to a town of
Galilee called Nazareth."*   *Luke 1:26*

MASTER artists have made the scene of the
Annunciation familiar to us. Yet the important
thing in their portrait of an angel and a girl is
altogether hidden: Jesus incarnate in the womb of
Mary. This hidden, intimate union is the world's
First Holy Communion. It was God-made-man,
Redemption's first stirring, Mary's divine Motherhood. But it was also Mary's Lord in her humble
heart, pouring His grace down upon the lovely
pastures of her soul.

My soul is meant to grow in grace. Christ feeds
it with Himself, cultivating His divine life in me.
What a gift Eucharist is to me.

II. THE VISITATION

"The hungry he has filled with good things."
Luke 1:53

IN the very first days of her pregnancy, Mary visited her cousin Elizabeth's home. There it was that she sang "Magnificat." In this sudden song of the praise of God, she tells me a secret about my soul's food: "God fills the hungry." Mary wanted God, hungered after God, and God entrusted His Son to her care. God heaped "good things" on the table of her heart – His Son. Jesus, "the fruit of her womb," was divine fruit for her soul.

Christ in the Eucharist is my soul's food. Jesus fills my emptiness and satisfies my insatiable hunger.

III. THE BIRTH OF OUR LORD

*"You will find an infant wrapped in swaddling clothes
and lying in a manger."*   Luke 2:12

THE "good news" of Christmas was this: God
had come into the world. Good news indeed, but
Mary herself would never have known without an
angel's foretelling. Jesus in her arms in the cold
cave of Bethlehem was a very human baby. No
thunder down from Sinai, His thin little cry! This
tiny hand does it hold stars in place? This Infant-
infinite? See, the cattle in the cave bend no knee;
the air is not suddenly fragrant; no heavenly lights
mellow the hard, unfriendly darkness. Very human
is Mary's Child, beyond our understanding.

Humanity and divinity – the Eucharist is both.

IV. THE PRESENTATION IN THE TEMPLE

"Simeon was righteous and devout, awaiting the consolation of Israel and the Holy Spirit was upon him."
                                              Luke 2:25

THE Eucharist was not without prophets. Miraculous manna sustaining the Israelites in their wanderings; hearthcakes of Elias, who "walked in the strength of that food forty days." Now, in the mystery of the Presentation, another quiet foreshadowing, rather two. Mary gives her Son to the priest; the priest offers Him to the Father – the gift of the Infant Jesus! Mary gives her Son to Simeon, who "received Him and blessed God." Longed-for "communion," fervent thanksgiving – prophets of the secret of the saints!

It was Mary who gave Jesus to the priest, Simeon. Holy Communion with God comes through her gift.

V. THE FINDING OF THE CHILD JESUS IN THE TEMPLE

"After three days, they found him in the temple."
Luke 2:46

MARY and Joseph took their sorrow into the temple. There they found Jesus. That is why this is a Joyful Mystery. They had come to their kinsfolk and acquaintances, sorrowing; and sorrowing, they went away. Dumb with grief, they returned to the city. A hundred inquiries and a hundred crushing disappointments; false leads and heavier hearts; kind suggestions and cruel failures, until they took their sorrow into the temple where they found Jesus and "rejoiced over the lamb that was lost."

Worry, petty annoyances, discouragement, fear of the future – I'm no stranger to any of them. Jesus Christ wants to hear about them to ease my mind. I'll find Him in my heart, in my neighbor, in the Eucharist.

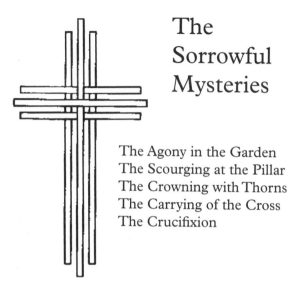

The Sorrowful Mysteries

The Agony in the Garden
The Scourging at the Pillar
The Crowning with Thorns
The Carrying of the Cross
The Crucifixion

EVIL

Our Lady will give us a deeper understanding of
evil through the five Sorrowful Mysteries

—one—
Our Father, Who art in Heaven...
—ten—
Hail Mary, full of grace...
—one—
Glory be to the Father...

79

I. THE AGONY IN THE GARDEN

"Are you the Son of God? He replied, 'You say that I am.'"   Luke 22:70

SELF will begins with the story of Adam and Eve. Adorned with a brilliant variety of graces and perfection, they gave them all up because of pride. Luckily, evil had no such success with Jesus in the desert. Thrice tempting and three times rebuked, "the devil fled from Him, and angels came to serve Him." Now, in the Garden of Olives, temptation reappears with innumerable fears. Twelve legions of angels are Christ's for the asking, but He is content to let events take their course and his enemies do as they will with Him.

Christ's death was evil. But God turned it into complete success. God help me turn my self will into your will.

II. THE SCOURGING AT THE PILLAR

"Simon, Simon, Satan desires to sift you like wheat."
Luke 22:31

PETER was a puzzle to the demon. Weak, precipitous Peter, all his courage in his tongue; yet, "you are the rock," Jesus had said to him, "and upon you, the rock, I will raise up My Church and hell itself shall not withstand it!" Salt on Satan's wounded pride – this country braggart, who couldn't catch fish without Jesus' help, whose faith survived just five steps upon the waters, whom Jesus Himself had often rebuked for "not savoring the things of God"; this the rock that will survive the storms of hell? Satan must do more than kill Christ; he must sift the rock as wheat.

Satan helped Peter to deny Christ. Evil will try to overcome me too. Jesus help me.

III. THE CROWNING WITH THORNS

"They clothed him in purple and, weaving a crown of thorns, placed it on Him."   *Mark 15:17*

SATAN'S temptation ruined Adam and Eve; but pride had first ruined Satan. Placed among the highest angelic spirits, destined to be light-bearer before the throne of God, he nonetheless threw the whole of his mighty will into a single act of disobedience, too calculated for repentance. Perhaps the mystery of the coming Incarnation was revealed to him, and he could not bear to worship a God in lowly human form. If so, hell had its one moment of vengeance during the brutal ceremonial in Pilot's praetorium, when men "venerated" an Incarnate God as devils might do.

In Ephesians, Paul advises us to draw our strength from the Lord and from His mighty power. Put on the armor of God so that we may be able to stand firm against the tactics of the devil.

IV. THE CARRYING OF THE CROSS

"But this man has done nothing criminal."
                                    Luke 23:41

EVIL had exhausted its malice when Jesus died. Satan led Judas to his betrayal, Peter to his denial; then came the hour of the powers of darkness: false accusations, unjust trials, mockings, scourgings, then the cross. Evil could do no more, we would say. But Jesus knew better. Once He had told His surprised disciples, "Greater works than mine shall you do." Now, on the way to Calvary, He seems to warn the women who weep over His plight, "Greater sufferings than Mine shall you endure."

Today, good people are suffering in numbers as never before. Sin is afflicting the human race. Mary, we pray the Rosary as you requested at Fatima. Help me overcome the evil within me.

V. THE CRUCIFIXION

"When all the people who had gathered for this spectacle saw what had happened, they returned home beating their breasts."   *Luke 23:48*

FOR three hours, the dying Jesus hung on the cross. How often Jesus must have been tempted in His life. The Gospels tell us of His temptation in the desert. Jesus transcended them by refusing to presume upon His Father's power. Now borne high on Calvary, Jesus is again challenged: "Come down from the cross!" He refuses! Then Jesus dies, and the centurion cries aloud: "This is God's Son"; the temple curtain is ripped in two, the dead rise from their graves, heaven's gates open wide, and Jesus triumphantly leads a repentant thief into paradise.

Jesus' refusal to come down from the cross was His greatest victory. By accepting my life's crosses patiently, prayerfully, I transcend evil.

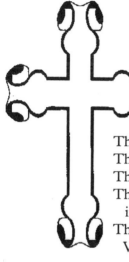

The Glorious Mysteries

The Resurrection
The Ascension of our Lord
The Descent of the Holy Spirit
The Assumption of our Lady
  into Heaven
The Coronation of the Blessed
  Virgin Mary

NEW LIFE IN CHRIST

Our Lady will give us a deeper understanding
of *new life in Christ* through the five Glorious
Mysteries

—one—
Our Father, Who art in Heaven...
—ten—
Hail Mary, full of grace...
—one—
Glory be to the Father...

85

I. THE RESURRECTION

"On the first day of the week, they took the spices they had prepared and went to the tomb."

Luke 24:1

FOR a night and a day and another night, the body of Jesus Christ lay in the tomb, a great stone at the door sealing in the darkness. The pale limbs were washed and wrapped in linen; a white cloth covered His face, a winding sheet with aromatic spices encircled His body. Bloodless, lifeless, unpleasant to see or think about ... Then, quick as thought, the frail grey body was alive again, and rose bright as a dozen suns!

Through Baptism, our souls, radiate divine grace. Just as "Christ rose and appeared to many," so should I appear to the world as a follower of Christ, radiating virtue.

II. THE ASCENSION OF OUR LORD

"I am baptizing you with water, for repentance, but the one who is coming after me is mightier than I."

Matthew 3:11

JOHN the Baptist was not merely the prophet of Christ; his life was a preview of Christ's. His birth was foretold by an angel: his father was troubled, his mother gave thanks. He lived a hidden life. His first words in public – "Do penance, the kingdom of God is at hand" – were Christ's as well. He was hated by the Pharisees. Human respect led Herod to order John's death, just as Pilate condemned Jesus for fear of the people. And John's baptism, though a symbol of repentance, foreshadowed Christ's sacrament which makes us temples of God and His children.

By Baptism, God lives in us; by a life of fidelity to grace, we shall live forever in God.

III. THE DESCENT OF THE HOLY SPIRIT

"Why are you terrified, O you of little faith?"
Matthew 8:26

THE Apostles were very brave as long as Jesus was a popular hero. "Let us go to Jerusalem and die with Him! Lord, we have been casting out devils! Master, shall we call down fire from heaven to destroy them? We can drink of thy chalice! I would die before disowning Thee!" But when the storm of hatred and revenge burst over Christ's head, the Apostles, after one wild stroke of the sword in His defense, fled like frightened deer. But after Pentecost – they begin to be glad to suffer for Christ.

Spirit of God fill me with your gifts: wisdom, counsel, courage, knowledge, understanding, humility, and love of God.

IV. THE ASSUMPTION OF OUR LADY INTO HEAVEN

"There were many women there, looking on from a distance – and the veil of the sanctuary was torn."
                                        Matthew 27:55, 51

SHE bore Him – body, soul, divinity – beneath her heart for nine months. For thirty-three years, He was her heart's preoccupation. Mary learned that spirituality meant living and loving as her Son taught. Mary knew Jesus so well. How does a mother survive the death of her child? Only her faith in the God her Son had made known to her could help.

She is a sign to all of us who experience such a great loss. She spent the remainder of her life being the mother of Jesus' Church.

Mary, help me to overcome my sorrow, rise above my pain and live for others.

V. THE CORONATION OF THE BLESSED VIRGIN MARY

"Woman, this is your son." Then to the disciple, "this is your mother."   *John 19:26-27*

THE Church gives us Mary as a model of true discipleship. She is the one who said "yes" to God and therefore allowed her will to be God's will. This is such a difficult thing for us to do. As human beings we get so busy with our lives and our desires that we often can't determine what it is God would have us do.

Mary is our mother. She waits for us to ask. Then she willingly joins us in our struggle to see God's will. She will help us learn to say "yes" to God. Mary, thank you for being my mother.

Personal Notes

The Joyful Mysteries

The Annunciation
The Visitation
The Birth of our Lord
The Presentation in the Temple
The Finding of the Child Jesus
  in the Temple

SPIRITUALITY

Our Lady will give us a deeper understanding of
spirituality through the five Joyful Mysteries

—one—
Our Father, Who art in Heaven...
—ten—
Hail Mary, full of grace...
—one—
Glory be to the Father...

I. THE ANNUNCIATION

"Now this is how the birth of Jesus Christ came about."   *Matthew 1:18*

GABRIEL, going from God to the Virgin Mary, merely exchanged one paradise for another. A sea of grace, Mary's soul, almost without shore, depth, horizon. So blessed was she – "The limits of the Infinite," one Church Father called her – that even the Lord God would become incarnate in her. The Virgin Mary, bright diamond set in the ring of all humanity, engaging heaven to earth.

But God is more mindful of His mercy than of His dignity. In every soul, the Blessed Trinity dwells, as truly, as in heaven, though unseen. I am not always near a church, but always I can pray to God in my soul.

II. THE VISITATION

"Blessed are you who believed that what was spoken to you by the Lord would be fulfilled."

Luke 1:45

ELIZABETH was with child in her old age – and even the townsfolk didn't know. According to Jewish custom, Elizabeth "secluded herself for five months"; and Zachary had been struck dumb for his doubting! The secret was, gratifyingly, all theirs. So they thought, until Mary came from Nazareth to congratulate them. But Mary's own secret must be given in exchange. Filled with the Holy Spirit, Elizabeth cried out, "Why should I be honored with a visit from the Mother of my Lord?"

By the light of the Holy Spirit, Elizabeth knew that Jesus was in Mary. Like Elizabeth, I can develop the habit of seeing Christ in my neighbor – a vital part of true Christian living. Prayerful devotion to the Holy Spirit, "the Spirit of Jesus," is the key.

III. THE BIRTH OF OUR LORD

"So they went in haste and found Mary and Joseph and the infant lying in the manger."

Luke 2:16

THE fullness of time. The Mother of God held the fruit of her womb wrapped in swaddling clothes – her arms filled with the harvest of her body. But this was not an autumn, not a completion, not the final brush stroke on a masterpiece. It was spring, the beginning of new things, the first unpretentious line across a canvas. Jesus had come to grow in wisdom, age, and strength, to teach, to redeem, and finally to sanctify those He had saved with His Spirit.

The Holy Spirit living in my soul is the ultimate purpose of Christmas. Bethlehem looked forward – to me.

IV. THE PRESENTATION IN THE TEMPLE

"Now, master, you may let your servant go in peace, according to your word."　　　　　*Luke 2:29*

SIMEON stood in the shadow of the temple gate, dim eyes dancing with expectation. He should have died long ago, this bearded ancient. But hope had tethered his soul; God had promised him sight of the Christ. Crowds passed him by; then he saw Joseph, and Mary holding Jesus. Common folk they were and the child like any other – as common as bread and wine. But Simeon stepped forward into the sunlight; his eyes had seen his salvation.

The Holy Spirit led Simeon to the temple and showed him God as a Child. My faith, too, is God's doing. God will lead me to see Jesus in others.

V. THE FINDING OF THE CHILD JESUS IN THE TEMPLE

"And Jesus advanced in wisdom and age and favor before God."   *Luke 2:52*

JESUS loved Mary and Joseph as only a Son who is God can love. Yet, without telling, He stayed behind in Jerusalem as they set out for Nazareth. He did not wish to hurt them, but it was "His Father's business." And so, Jesus remained in the temple, where Jesus felt God called him to stay.

Courage to do what God wants, whatever others may think – I need that every hour of the day. It is a gift of the Holy Spirit in my soul. Constant praying to Him will give me strength to do God's will perfectly.

The Sorrowful Mysteries

The Agony in the Garden
The Scourging at the Pillar
The Crowning with Thorns
The Carrying of the Cross
The Crucifixion

JUDAS

Our Lady will give us a deeper understanding of
Judas through the five Sorrowful Mysteries

—one—
Our Father, Who art in Heaven...
—ten—
Hail Mary, full of grace...
—one—
Glory be to the Father...

I. THE AGONY IN THE GARDEN

"While he was still speaking, a crowd approached and in front was one of the Twelve, a man named Judas."
                                              Luke 22:47

NO one who knew Jesus, heard Him speak, or watched miracles radiate from His compassionate power could remain indifferent to Him. If one did not love Jesus ardently, one hated Him. Even as a baby, He was hated by Herod who tried to murder Him; yet the Christ Child was loved by wiser men from the East. Pharisees hated Him with the cancerous malice bred of envy; the Apostles loved Him like little children. Even Judas loved Him. And, infinitely, Jesus loved Judas. The traitor's kiss in the Garden was more than a sign for the soldiers. What was Judas thinking?

Jesus said to him, "My friend, do what you are here for." Could Judas have known what he was doing? God help me to be aware of your will.

II. THE SCOURGING AT THE PILLAR

"I have sinned in betraying innocent blood."
Matthew 27:4

IN the early hours of Good Friday morning, Judas committed two great sins: He sold God the Son for silver; that was his first crime. Then, realizing the enormity of such an act, and with waves of remorse surging over his poor soul, he sinned again, with scarcely less enormity and with an eternal finality – he doubted the mercy of God, and despaired of forgiveness.

Judas could have become a great saint after betraying Jesus. Think of the heights of perfect humility he might have ascended had he turned to God for pardon.

Jesus, who called Judas "friend" in the Garden, is offended less by betrayal than by despair.

101

III. THE CROWNING WITH THORNS

"Whom are you looking for?"   *John 18:4*

MIDWAY through the Last Supper, evil entered Judas. St. John, reminiscing on the scene as he wrote his gospel, added a phrase that tells exactly the state of Judas' soul: "And now it was night." Blind to the arresting blend of meekness that he had once loved in Jesus, Judas' concerns had changed. Once the deed was done, however, sight was returned to his soul, and he saw his guilt with terrible clarity. "The price of Him" shining dully in his hand was too much for him to bear. He ran from the Temple and flung the thirty coins at the Pharisees' feet.

Judas turned away from Jesus; then he realized no earthly reward was worth the price. That is the way with sin. We turn from God and it leaves us empty.

IV. THE CARRYING OF THE CROSS

"He returned the thirty pieces of silver."

Matthew 27:3

WAS this a confession of his crime in all its
terrible malice – "I have sinned; I have betrayed
innocent blood." Did three years of close companionship finally open Judas' eyes to Christ's
radiant divinity? Did Jesus have to suffer before
Judas understood? But then, why did he despair?
Did he never realize how much Jesus loved him?

To realize *who* loves me when I commit sin is the
surest way to overcome temptation. I should pray
for a strong, living, practical faith in Jesus Christ,
the Son of God, who loves me more than life
itself.

V. THE CRUCIFIXION

*"Then was fulfilled what had been said through
Jeremiah the prophet, 'And they took thirty pieces of
silver...and paid it out for the potter's field just as the
Lord had commanded me.'"*

Matthew 27:9-10

JUDAS was an ambitious man. With many of his
contemporaries, he was awaiting the restoration
of Israel, God's kingdom on earth, and he was
shrewd enough to see that the wonder-working
Jesus could establish it. But Judas didn't care at
all for Christ's way of reigning on earth. He had
paid very close attention to Jesus' talk about the
cross and the blessings of poverty and he didn't
understand. So he took matters into his own
hands.

God, I am often ambitious. Guide me and be my
true wisdom. Let me be ambitious about doing
your will.

The Glorious Mysteries

The Resurrection
The Ascension of our Lord
The Descent of the Holy Spirit
The Assumption of our Lady
  into Heaven
The Coronation of the Blessed
  Virgin Mary

THE SACRAMENTS

Our Lady will give us a deeper understanding of
the *sacraments* through the five Glorious Mysteries

—one—
Our Father, Who art in Heaven...
—ten—
Hail Mary, full of grace...
—one—
Glory be to the Father...

105

I. THE RESURRECTION

*"The Anointing of the Sick completes the holy an-
nointings that mark the whole Christian life: that of
Baptism which sealed the new life in us, and that of
Confirmation."*   *Catechism, no. 1523*

FROM the time when Samuel anointed Saul as
the first king of the Jews, the leaders of the
Israelites were God's "anointed ones." They
waited for their anointed one, their Messiah. And
Jesus Christ, when He came, was anointed king
indeed – anointed with the Holy Spirit that every
knee in heaven and earth should bend before the
name Jesus. Jesus was also anointed by a woman
as He reclined at table with Simon the leper. She
poured out a vial of costly oil upon His head.

The anointing of the sick has wonderful effects
upon those who celebrate this sacrament. It unites
us in our sickness and pain with words of comfort
and the grace of peace of mind.

II. THE ASCENSION OF OUR LORD

"He took a towel and tied it around his waist...and began to wash their feet."   *John 13:4-5*

JUST before His Ascension, our Lord said to His Apostles, "You are to be my witnesses." As the Church, we continue to bring the Reign of God into being. Through the Sacrament of Holy Orders, the ordained preside at the Eucharist and preach God's word. They are given the task, along with the people of God, of introducing Jesus to the world. The pope, cardinals, bishops, priests, and deacons are the servants of the Church. It is through their example we are to learn to wash each other's feet.

Mary, help your sons to be more like Jesus in all they do. Teach us to support each other in our vocations in life.

III. THE DESCENT OF THE HOLY SPIRIT

"I have given you a model to follow, so that as I have done for you, you should also do."

John 13:15

IN Old Testament times, the chief office of the Jewish priest was to offer sacrifice to God – rams, fatlings, the scapegoat, first fruits of the harvest, the Paschal lamb. It was a ritual act for the people of Israel, it symbolized God making the covenant real once again.

We have always known we are entirely dependent on God – rituals renew our belief that God chooses to be in a covenant relationship with us. We have always asked the head of our community to preside at these rituals.

Jesus is our perfect sacrament, our perfect sacrifice. God, never let us doubt your perfect love.

IV. THE ASSUMPTION OF OUR LADY INTO HEAVEN

"The intimate community of life and love which constitutes the married state has been established by the Creator."   *Catechism, no. 1603*

IN the story of Eden, Adam had God above him to love and all creation below him to rule and delight in. But he had no one, at first, to share his happiness. "Not good," said God; and out of Adam came Eve to be his bride, and the mother of our race. Thousands of years after, in a setting by no means paradisial, God was born of a woman – in a Bethlehem cave; Jesus was born of Mary. And Jesus, Mary, and Joseph became a Holy Family.

On Calvary, this Mother of Jesus became the Mother of the Church. The Church and Jesus have a relationship that is eternal.

The Sacrament of Matrimony reflects the sacred union of Christ and the Church. Jesus, Mary and the Church are eager to support those who live the sacrament of matrimony. Surely, we need their help.

V. THE CORONATION OF THE BLESSED VIRGIN MARY

"By reason of their state in life...they help one another to attain holiness in their married life."

Catechism, no. 1641

WITH omnipotent ease, simply by willing what He had thought upon, God created all things out of nothingness. Compared with Him, the star-laden universe is no more spectacular than a kicked-up cloud of dust. But on one of those specks of dust, the Earth, He has fastened His loving attention. It is the home of His favorite children: us. So much does God love the human race that He himself became a man that we might have eternal life. And though we can do absolutely nothing by ourselves, God has given us a mighty power with everlasting consequences. We have the power to become God's children.

Those who enter the vocation of marriage are called upon to help one another and their families become God's children. Mary, mother of us all, we ask for your guidance.

Personal Notes

The
Joyful
Mysteries

The Annunciation
The Visitation
The Birth of our Lord
The Presentation in the Temple
The Finding of the Child Jesus
    in the Temple

PROVIDENCE

Our Lady will give us a deeper understanding of
providence through the five Joyful Mysteries

—one—
Our Father, Who art in Heaven...
—ten—
Hail Mary, full of grace...
—one—
Glory be to the Father...

113

I. THE ANNUNCIATION

"Hail, favored one! The Lord is with you."
                                        Luke 1:28

AS a child, Mary had vowed her virginity to God, and gone was any earthly hope of becoming the Savior's mother. Other Jewish maidens might cherish such an honor. But Mary's love for God was so great it did not even occur to her that she was renouncing anything. She simply loved God and left everything else to Him. That is how she became the Mother of God.

Mary was totally abandoned to God's Providence, and God did impossible things for her. I am in the palm of His hand; when things seem darkest, it is God's hand closing over me – "the power of the Most High shall overshadow thee."

Total confidence in God – my happy obligation!

II. THE VISITATION

"For at the moment that the sound of thy greeting reached my ears, the infant in my womb leaped for joy."   *Luke 1:44*

THE Savior must have a mother worthy of Him; that is why God created Mary immaculate. His precursor, John the Baptist, should have credentials proportioned to his office. John was filled with the Holy Spirit even from his mother's womb, by Christ himself, whom the Virgin Mary had just conceived by the Holy Spirit. She greeted her aged cousin with warm affection, and at her words, sanctifying grace poured into the soul of Elizabeth's unborn child.

God cares for all, from the least things to the great events of the world. That is the meaning of God's providence. Caring for my family, my friends, my faith, my talents, my duties, my circumstances – that is God's will for me.

III. THE BIRTH OF OUR LORD

"There was no room for them in the inn."

Luke 2:7

THIS is a Joyful Mystery, but not a comfortable one. The hilly, hundred-mile journey from Nazareth to Bethlehem was always tiring and often dangerous, and Mary was but a few days from childbirth when she made it. Bethlehem, King David's town, was host, seemingly, to all of David's descendants. The courtyard inn was prosperously overcrowded, with room for more; but no room for Mary. The best that Joseph could do for her was a dark, damp, ill-smelling cave. Drama there was none; they were just cold and tired, and at peace. And in this place, God was born.

Some people call pleasant things "providential." Mary and Joseph thought everything was. God is in everything and every place. Nothing is without God. A truth for me to live by!

IV. THE PRESENTATION IN THE TEMPLE

"Blessed are you who are poor for the Kingdom of God is yours."   *Luke 6:20*

ANNA was something of a local phenomenon in Jerusalem. Everyone knew the story: how, as a young widow, she had come to the temple one day to pray, and had been there, praying and fasting, ever since for all of sixty years! She had always been there. They used to say she was more than a celebrity; she was a tradition. Simeon was neither. He was only "some old man down by the gate"; everyone had seen him, but no one took note of him. Providence chose both, Anna, the temple figure, and Simeon of no reknown, as the Savior's childhood prophets.

Providence still "chooses both"; the "nobodies" and "somebodies" are equally the instruments of God. His plans for me depend on what I am inside.

117

V. THE FINDING OF THE CHILD JESUS IN THE TEMPLE

"And I tell you, ask and you will receive; seek and you will find."   *Luke 11:9*

MARY had walked many times along the "strange ways" of Providence. An angel had proclaimed her God's Virgin Mother; a skyful of angels had caroled the birth of her Son; a new star brought Magi to His feet; Simeon's bittersweet prophecies were still her daily bread. But now Mary was just a mother who had lost her boy. She waited not a minute for angel or prophet. She began to look for Jesus. No one ever trusted as Mary did, and no one ever searched as hard as she.

God saw to it that Jesus was returned to His Mother – after she had searched for Him. God provides – if I provide!

The Sorrowful Mysteries

The Agony in the Garden
The Scourging at the Pillar
The Crowning with Thorns
The Carrying of the Cross
The Crucifixion

RECONCILIATION

Our Lady will give us a deeper understanding of *reconciliation* through the five Sorrowful Mysteries

—one—
Our Father, Who art in Heaven...
—ten—
Hail Mary, full of grace...
—one—
Glory be to the Father...

119

I. THE AGONY IN THE GARDEN

"Blessed are those whom the master finds vigilant on his arrival."   Luke 12:37

JESUS loved to be with His Apostles and to preach to the multitudes; but He also loved to be alone with His Father. The Apostles were used to seeing Him leave their company after sunset, to spend His nights by Himself on a mountainside, praying. They talked about it among themselves and, when not too tired, wished they could accompany Him. They had their chance at last on Holy Thursday night; Jesus invited Peter, James, and John to watch and pray with Him on Mount Olivet. And they failed Him. He rose from His agony and found them asleep.

Many in our world are in agony. Many feel alone and abandoned. Can you not watch one hour with them?

II. THE SCOURGING AT THE PILLAR

"You say I am a King, for this I came into the world, to testify to the truth."
                                                              John 18:37

NOT the least of Christ's miracles was His continual escape from physical suffering at the hands of His enemies. Divine intervention had prevented the death of the Christ Child, and He came to no harm even in the land of Egypt. His fellow townsmen, angered by His first sermon in the synagogue, dragged Him off to a high cliff to do away with Him, "but He departed from their midst." Even when the elements seemed to conspire against Him as He crossed the storm-swept Sea of Galilee, Jesus slept unconcernedly. But it was quite otherwise on Good Friday, when Roman soldiers tied Him to a post and lashed His Body to ribbons.

It is impossible to avoid suffering for long. But we must always remember that God is present in the brokenness and emptiness of our situation.

III. THE CROWNING WITH THORNS

"Simon, son of John, do you love me more than these?"   *John 21:15*

WHILE Jesus was being beaten, while the soldiers scoffed and Pharisees exulted, while the people called Christ's blood upon their heads, one man wept and wept. In a lonely corner of the city, or perhaps in the seclusion of Olivet, broken-hearted Peter cried his heart's blood out at the thought of what he had done to Jesus. How proud he had been that day a year ago when he said to Jesus, "Thou are the Christ, the Son of the living God." Peter had been the first to confess Christ; now he was the first to deny Him. Like Judas, he might have gone out and hanged himself; instead, he went out and wept.

Judas was desperately sorry; Peter was humbly contrite. The heart of reconciliation is believing in God's mercy.

IV. THE CARRYING OF THE CROSS

"Whoever finds his life will lose it, and whoever loses his life for my sake will find it."

Matthew 10:39

A woman followed Jesus as He made His slow way to Calvary. Her eyes betrayed her anxiety to draw near to Jesus. It was not an easy thing to do. The guards surrounding Jesus wasted no courtesy on the crowd that milled about; when a passerby delayed the procession, a soldier's sword spun him out of the way. Still the woman followed; and her chance came. Jesus fell on His face; the soldiers busied themselves in flogging Him to His feet, and were even grudgingly grateful when Veronica ran up and wiped Jesus' face with her veil.

Veronica's small service was heroic because it was done for Christ. By offering my thoughts, words, and actions to God often during the day, I turn them into "Veronica's veils" for the suffering body of Christ, His Church.

V. THE CRUCIFIXION

"In the beginning was the Word and the Word was with God and the Word was God."   *John 1:1*

THE mere listing of Jesus' suffering in His Passion seems to exhaust the possibilities of human misfortune. In such agony, He sweated blood. Betrayed, denied, deserted, arrested, falsely accused, condemned unjustly, blindfolded, spat upon, beaten, ridiculed by Herod, scourged by Pilate, crowned with thorns, loaded with the cross and then nailed to it, he endured utter abandonment and even death.

Our sickness and pain may be different than His – but that does not separate us from God. There is no pain or suffering of which God is not a part. That is the meaning of the Cross.

God, sometimes I feel so alone – let me remember you are with me.

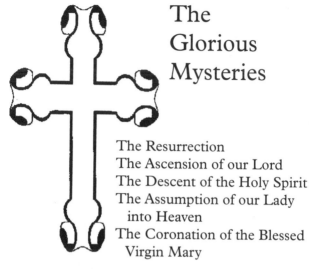

The Glorious Mysteries

The Resurrection
The Ascension of our Lord
The Descent of the Holy Spirit
The Assumption of our Lady
   into Heaven
The Coronation of the Blessed
   Virgin Mary

PURGATORY

Our Lady will give us a deeper understanding of *purgatory* through the five Glorious Mysteries

—one—
Our Father, Who art in Heaven...
—ten—
Hail Mary, full of grace...
—one—
Glory be to the Father...

125

I. THE RESURRECTION

"When it says, 'he ascended,' what can it mean if not that he descended right down to the lower regions of the earth? The one who rose higher than all the heavens to fill all things is none other than the one who descended."

Ephesians 4:9-10

THERE were many holy people before the time of Christ, but no saints. That is, the Church had not named them as saints. Between His death and Resurrection, Jesus visited these souls. "The Apostles' Creed confesses in the same article Christ's descent into hell and his Resurrection from the dead on the third day, because in His Passover it was precisely out of the depth of death that he made life spring forth." (Catechism, no. 631) There, in the dwelling of the dead, Jesus preached the dawning of eternal life.

Jesus, help us to understand and accept your great gift of love.

II. THE ASCENSION OF OUR LORD

"They have taken the Lord from the tomb and we don't know where they put him."   *John 20:2*

ONE of the mysteries of Calvary was the twin presence of the Beatific Vision and the most terrible suffering. Christ on the cross, drinking from the fountains of life while dying in terrible thirst; lost in bliss at the sight of His Father, yet crying out, "My God, why hast Thou forsaken me?"; bathed in the light of God, yet preyed upon by the powers of darkness. This great mystery of the Cross is the mystery of purgatory. What is this place? Is it a place of suffering? We believe that God is completely just and merciful. Since the Council of Trent, the Church has taught that in this place we are detained after death and helped by all the prayers of the faithful.

Mary, be with us at the hour of our death.

III. THE DESCENT OF THE HOLY SPIRIT

"And they were all filled with the Holy Spirit."
                                                    Acts 2:4

JESUS did not choose for His Apostles men of iron wills. He chose (as God always does choose) "the weak things of the earth." He chose Peter, who "savored not the things of God," and denied His master thrice. He chose James and John, who wanted the first two places in heaven. He chose Philip who after three years did not recognize the Heavenly Father in Jesus. He chose Judas, who sold Him for thirty pieces of silver. Weak, untrustworthy, timorous, sinful men, the Apostles – until Pentecost. Then, divine fire came down upon them, and they went forth "rejoicing to suffer for the name of Jesus."

Jesus, I am also weak, but I want to serve you. Make me strong.

IV. THE ASSUMPTION OF OUR LADY INTO HEAVEN

"The Assumption of the Blessed Virgin is a singular participation in her Son's Resurrection and an anticipation of the resurrection of other Christians."

Catechism, no. 966

THE Mother of God died of love. God had poured so much love for Himself into her soul that at last she could not contain it without having Him as well. So she died. We do not know if she felt the weakness of old age, or disease, or physical suffering. Losing her son was a pain of love. When her soul had reached its incomparable perfection, God took her up to heaven, as one might pick a lovely flower in full-bloom. Mary's love for God and God's love for Mary brought her, pure body and soul, to be with God forever.

Love causes the deepest pain. What was true for Mary is true for the souls in purgatory. It is their growing love for God that brings them joy and pain.

V. THE CORONATION OF THE BLESSED VIRGIN MARY

*"She is clearly the mother of the members of Christ...
since she has by her charity joined in bringing about
the birth of believers in the Church."*

Catechism, no. 963

MARY had been given many wonderful privileges: for example, her Immaculate Conception and her initial fullness of grace. The seven stars about her head are her Seven Sorrows, their splendor outshone only by her Son's glorious wounds. Her role in relation to the Church and to all humanity goes further than privilege. "In a wholly singular way she cooperated by her obedience, faith, hope, and burning charity in the Savior's work of restoring supernatural life to souls. For this reason she is a mother to us in the order of grace." (Lumen Gentium, 53, 63)

Mary, teach me faith, hope and burning charity.

131

Personal Notes

The Joyful Mysteries

The Annunciation
The Visitation
The Birth of our Lord
The Presentation in the Temple
The Finding of the Child Jesus in
   the Temple

THE CHURCH

Our Lady will give us a deeper understanding of the *Church* through the five Joyful Mysteries

—one—
Our Father, Who art in Heaven...
—ten—
Hail Mary, full of grace...
—one—
Glory be to the Father...

I. THE ANNUNCIATION

"Jesus is the Messiah, the Son of God, and through this belief you may have life in His name."

John 20:31

"THE Lord is with thee." Mary was the Mother of God. Surely that was enough for now; let Gabriel tell it, and quietly go away. But Gabriel had more to tell; Mary was to hear everything at once. A windfall of wonders; God would be her Son. She would be a Virgin Mother. The Lord would give her Son the throne of David. He would rule over the house of Jacob. His reign would have no end. From the dawn of her Motherhood, Mary knew this child would be great – she learned His greatness would become the Church and would never end.

Jesus and the Church form "the whole Christ." Mary is my Mother; and she loves me with the love she has for Jesus. She wants me to love her Son totally.

II. THE VISITATION

"He was in the beginning with God."

John 1:2

THE Incarnation was not the mere placing of an event; it was a prophecy, the flower's foretelling. The Incarnation prophesied Pentecost; the angel spoke to Mary emphatically of the Church, and the Holy Spirit descended upon her. The Visitation caught up this Pentecostal theme. Elizabeth was already six months with child, the angel had said; and Mary hurried off to attend her. Mary was to do more than she realized. She spoke, and John was filled with sanctifying grace. Mary, Apostle to her Son's Precursor!

Mary has one desire in heaven: that the Catholic Church – the "whole Christ" – should grow on earth. Her heart is an apostle's heart. Is mine?

III. THE BIRTH OF OUR LORD

"If you remain in my word, you will truly be my disciples and you will know the truth, and the truth will set you free."

John 8:31-32

ENVYING the Magi must have been an easy vice. In a land that worshipped wisdom, they were wisest. Wealth was theirs, and, what the East covets more, the respectability of virtue. But the Magi were not happy men. They were too wise to rest content with merely human wisdom. Death would spend their money in a moment; virtue was not its own reward. That is why they went out of the East to Bethlehem. They had "everything under the sun" but they needed what was under their star. They needed Jesus Christ.

Do I live the kind of life that will attract others? Do I show others the Christ the Magi found under that star?

IV. THE PRESENTATION IN THE TEMPLE

"I am the light of the world."

John 8:12

MARY and Joseph went unnoticed past the doctors of the law, seated in well-attended groups along the temple colonnade. Professional champions of the law and prophets, they preached the chosen race and ignored the Gentiles for whose sake the race was chosen. Minimizing the prophets, they had conjured up a Savior whose mission was revenge on Rome. That is why Mary and Joseph did not stop along the colonnade, but gave the Child Jesus into the arms of Simeon, a quiet old man with a world vision.

A Catholic without "world vision" is a contradiction. "Catholic" means "world-wide." Prayer is a worldwide apostolate; a daily Rosary said by people all over the world will make us a world at peace.

V. THE FINDING OF THE CHILD JESUS IN THE TEMPLE

"I know where I came from and where I am going."

Luke 2:52

HALF a thousand times had the prophets spoken directly of the Christ to come. His personality, life, teaching, death, kingdom – nothing escaped their inspired vision. The Savior would have to prove His claim "according to the prophets." Without this self-vindication, He deserved no hearing. That is why, even as a boy of twelve, Jesus introduced Himself to the temple servants listening intently, suggesting possibilities, giving soul to the law, synthesizing the prophets. Jesus had begun to vindicate the Christ.

Faith is a gift of God, but a gift wrapped in reason. Do I know why I believe in the "whole Christ": Jesus and the Church? Do I "have a reason for the faith that is in me?"

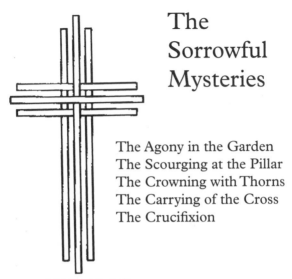

The Sorrowful Mysteries

The Agony in the Garden
The Scourging at the Pillar
The Crowning with Thorns
The Carrying of the Cross
The Crucifixion

THE PHARISEES

Our Lady will give us a deeper understanding of
the *Pharisees* through the five Sorrowful Mysteries

—one—
Our Father, Who art in Heaven...
—ten—
Hail Mary, full of grace...
—one—
Glory be to the Father...

I. THE AGONY IN THE GARDEN

"What is that to us?"   *Mathew 27:4*

IRONICALLY, the man who forced the Pharisees to admit their malice was not Jesus, but Judas. The conspirators were still in the temple arranging the morning trial, when an utterly broken Judas, so different from the shrewd, business-like traitor of an hour before appeared before them. "I have betrayed innocent blood!" he cried. Perhaps he expected a word of consolation from his partners-in-crime: "No, no, you did the right thing, Judas. God will bless you for it." Instead, he hears a frank confession of their deliberate blind hatred: "Innocent blood? What is that to us?"

The Pharisees tried to hide their guilt from Jesus, but made light of it before Judas. Is there some of that duplicity in me? Forgive me.

II. THE SCOURGING AT THE PILLAR

"And they themselves did not enter the praetorium, in order not to be defiled so that they could eat the Passover."   John 18:28

IF that sentence had not been written under God's inspiration, we would not believe such hypocrisy possible. This was the state of the Pharisees' hearts: they knew Jesus was what He claimed to be – the innocent Son of God; deliberately, in the bright daylight of this unwelcome conviction, they were proceeding to kill Him; yet, to avoid a purely legal defilement, they demanded that His trial be conducted outside the heathen Pilate's palace. Murder was an easy crime for them, but they would not break a rubric of the law.

The Pharisees were fussy about the trifles, but they didn't mind crucifying Christ. Am I altogether free from such self-deception?

141

III. THE CROWNING WITH THORNS

"We have no king but Caesar."　　　*John 19:15*

THE lies came easy for the Pharisees on Good Friday. They had bought Christ for cash, then judged Him worthy of death at their proceedings. Now, before Pilate, they spat out lie after lie about their prisoner. Jesus had once declared publicly, "I have come to save Israel's lost sheep"; and Pharisees tell Pilate, "We found Him perverting our nation." Jesus had once commanded, "Give to Caesar the things of Caesar": and the Pharisees tell Pilate, "He forbade us to pay Caesar tribute." Then these proud Jewish leaders, who detested their Roman conquerors, crowned their case against Christ their King with a supreme lie, "We have no king but Caesar."

A hypocrite is, at bottom, a liar. Am I truthful with others, and with myself?

IV. THE CARRYING OF THE CROSS

"Whether Jews or Greeks...we were all given to drink of one Spirit."   *1 Corinthians 12:13*

FIVE days before, the people of Jerusalem had sung Hosannas around the kingly figure of Christ; now Jesus heard them shout for His death. These people (like Peter) acted more through fear than malice.

Unjustly, the Jewish people still suffer. This anti-Semitism is a terrible crime for a Christian. As a Catholic, I must remember that I adore a God who, in becoming man, was born a Jew of a Jewish maiden, Mary.

V. THE CRUCIFIXION

"They answered and said to him, 'Our father is Abraham.' Jesus said to them, 'If you were Abraham's children, you would be doing the works of Abraham.'"

John 8:39

SOME of the world's most beautiful poetry was written by the Jewish prophets. Beside their lavish descriptions of the coming kingdom of the Messiah, the ancient land flowering with milk and honey – even Eden itself – seemed a desert by comparison. And the Pharisees, pouring over the prophets' lyrical lines, took their imagery literally. That is why Jesus was a stumbling block to these people. They wanted a Savior who would make earth a heaven; and they crucified Christ when He said, "My kingdom is not of this world."

"If you are the Son of God, come off the cross!" say the Pharisees. "If you are the children of God, take up the cross," says Jesus. My key to the kingdom of God is the cross of Jesus Christ.

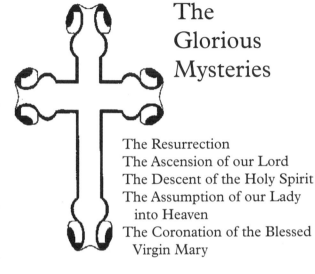

The Glorious Mysteries

The Resurrection
The Ascension of our Lord
The Descent of the Holy Spirit
The Assumption of our Lady
    into Heaven
The Coronation of the Blessed
    Virgin Mary

REIGN OF GOD

Our Lady will give us a deeper understanding of the *reign of God* through the five Glorious Mysteries

—one—
Our Father, Who art in Heaven...
—ten—
Hail Mary, full of grace...
—one—
Glory be to the Father...

145

I. THE RESURRECTION

"I am the way and the truth and the life."

John 14:6

JESUS Christ came to earth to show us the way to God the Father. He commanded those who wished to live holy lives "to hear the word of God and put it into practice." Jesus did not only point out the way to the Father; He is the Way. Jesus is our road to God, and all our strength for the journey comes from Him. I am the living bread which comes down from heaven, anyone who eats this bread will live forever, the Son of God says. And when we have reached the end of this divine path, we shall find the Bread of Life.

The more I love Jesus Christ now, the more the reign of God will be realized.

II. THE ASCENSION OF OUR LORD

"I think that what we suffer in this life can never be compared to the glory as yet unrevealed which is waiting for us."   Romans 8:18

THE Apostle Paul, who has told us so much about our faith, made no attempt to describe heaven. "What God prepared for those who love Him – well, eye hath not seen the like . . ." We cannot have an adequate idea of what happens after death. We imagine what it will be like for the three divine persons to fill our hearts and minds with Themselves. Mere ideas about God, which must content us on earth, will not come between God and ourselves in the next life. We shall know and love God and that is beyond our imagination.

The world that God created is filled with beauty and wonder – how much more beautiful will be what is to come!

III. THE DESCENT OF THE HOLY SPIRIT

"Love is patient."   *1 Corinthians 13:4*

THINK of God's patience! Nothing disturbs Him, nothing provokes Him, nothing excites Him. He has been sinned against a million times. Why does He continue to forgive us? Because He sees us, not only as we are, but as we shall be. God was patient with the dull-witted, blustery Apostles because, on Good Friday, Pentecost was before His eyes. And God is patient with me, and will be until I die, because He sees me already perfect in heaven.

In heaven, I will be perfect, and perfectly happy, forever. If that fact makes God patient with me, it should make me patient with myself and with others.

Lord, help me to love others as you love me.

IV. THE ASSUMPTION OF OUR LADY INTO HEAVEN

"It is the whole human person that is intended to become, in the body of Christ, a temple of the Spirit."

Catechism, no. 364

MARY is with God, body and soul. For her the second coming is already a reality. The light of glory that now fills her soul will pour out over all of us, transforming us, doing away with the heaviness, the sluggishness, the defects of sickness and death that make the body such a burden on earth. Instead it will shine as the sun; it will move quickly as thought; and all our senses, spiritualized and refined, will have their eternal fill of delight.

Our bodies will return to dust, so it is unwise to pamper them. But they will rise again in glory, so it is wrong to neglect them.

V. THE CORONATION OF THE BLESSED VIRGIN MARY

"The prayer of the church is sustained by the prayer of Mary and united with it in hope."

Catechism, no. 2679

MARY was humble and modest – but she was never withdrawn. When she heard that Elizabeth would bear a child, "she went with haste" to attend to her cousin's needs. Mary would have stayed with the crowd in the Bethlehem inn, but "there was no room." She went to Jerusalem with her neighbors. Everyone knew her: "Is not this the carpenter's Son, whose Mother is Mary?" She made the way of the cross with the crowd, and stood on Calvary with her sister and John and the Magdalene. She was with the Apostles on Pentecost; she mothered the infant Church. In heaven, too, she enjoys the company of all the angels and saints.

The Kingdom of God is a perfect society. God is the Father, Mary the Mother, of a family of numberless souls.

151

Personal Notes

The Joyful Mysteries

The Annunciation
The Visitation
The Birth of our Lord
The Presentation in the Temple
The Finding of the Child Jesus
    in the Temple

FAITH

Our Lady will give us a deeper understanding of
faith through the five Joyful Mysteries

—one—
Our Father, Who art in Heaven...
—ten—
Hail Mary, full of grace...
—one—
Glory be to the Father...

153

I. THE ANNUNCIATION

"The angel Gabriel was sent from God...to a virgin betrothed to a man named Joseph."

Luke 1:26-27

GOD sends Mary an angel. That rather spoils my meditation. Conversation with an angel – no lesson in faith, that! Actually, our response to such an extraordinary event would be precisely the reverse of Mary's reaction. Imperfect faith would have accepted the angel's astonishing message without question, gullibly; and afterwards questioned the whole apparition as a delusion. Mary, however, accepted the vision, and questioned only how the message would be fulfilled! "How shall this be done?" Then, reassured by the angel's explanation, she uttered her exquisite act of faith: "Be it done to me according to thy word."

God sent me an angel – no delusion! The message of God is brought to me through the daily Scriptures and the traditions of the Church. Praying the Rosary increases my faith.

II. THE VISITATION

"Blessed are you who believed that what was spoken to you by the Lord would be fulfilled."

Luke 1:45

THE Visitation was the linking of two swift dramas, strikingly alike save for the climax. The angel Gabriel had appeared to Zachary and Mary. To Zachary, ministering in the temple, he revealed that Elizabeth would conceive a son. Zachary asked, "How shall I know this? For I am an old man, and my wife is advanced in years." To Mary, praying in her home, Gabriel revealed that she was to conceive a Son. Mary asked, "How shall this happen, since I know not man?" Similar settings, revelation, questions in both scenes; yet Zachary disbelieved and Mary had absolute faith. Zachary's question was a refusal to believe; Mary's, a desire to understand.

Asking questions about the Church's mysteries, as Mary did, will confirm my faith.

III. THE BIRTH OF OUR LORD

"Then the shepherds returned, glorifying and praising God for all they had heard and seen, just as it had been told to them."   *Luke 2:20*

COLORLESS the cave certainly was, but signs and wonders filled the sky all around. Shepherds keeping a drowsy eye on their flocks were struck awake by the sudden chorus of angels' voices. "In the town of David, a Savior in a manger!" That was heaven's cue; across the clear sky, every star became a thousand angels, bright as suns, making melody for the Child in a cave. God had robbed the prince to pay the court; had surrounded the commonest Christmas Present with wrappings of Gold.

Appearances do deceive. God in a manger is a far greater wonder than angels in the sky. Faith puts me in contact with reality.

IV. THE PRESENTATION IN THE TEMPLE

"It is like a mustard seed... "   *Luke 13:19*

MARY'S faith was intense, past comprehension. At first, however, it concentrated upon a few truths: her Son was God, Savior, King. This was the faith-content of a child; Mary had much yet to learn. And Simeon had much to foretell: That her Son would be "a light for revelation to the Gentiles and glory for your people Israel." He would be the making and breaking of the world; that her own heart would be broken. Mary was learning; she "marveled at the things spoken of Him."

Mary began with few truths, but immense faith. I have every truth – and much less faith. To pray for stronger faith is to obtain stronger faith.

V. THE FINDING OF THE CHILD JESUS IN THE TEMPLE

"Increase our faith."   *Luke 17:5*

BEING the Mother of God certainly had its hardships! What was Mary supposed to say to Jesus when she finally found Him, calmly sitting among temple doctors? She could not scold Him. He was hers out of sheerest mercy, and of course He could not have done wrong. Still, she was His mother, and He obviously had not been searching Jerusalem for her! With a deep, helpless sigh, "Son, why hast Thou done so to us?" He answered something about "My Father's business" and even asked why she had bothered to look for Him! "The Lord had spoken" – but Mary did not understand.

God is "beyond me" too. He often does or permits things which make me ask, "Why has Thou done so to me?" The answer can only be found in faith.

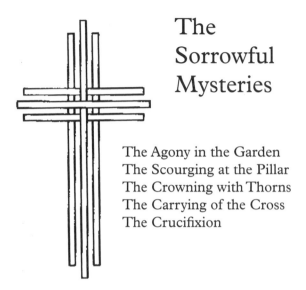

The Sorrowful Mysteries

The Agony in the Garden
The Scourging at the Pillar
The Crowning with Thorns
The Carrying of the Cross
The Crucifixion

LONELINESS

Our Lady will give us a deeper understanding of *loneliness* through the five Sorrowful Mysteries

—one—
Our Father, Who art in Heaven...
—ten—
Hail Mary, full of grace...
—one—
Glory be to the Father...

I. THE AGONY IN THE GARDEN

*"And to strengthen him an angel from heaven
appeared to him."*   Luke 22:43

LONELINESS – the feeling that one is without
comfort or understanding from others – was the
lot of Jesus Christ throughout His public life. "He
came unto His own, and they received Him not."
Even those who did receive Him often deserve to
hear Him say: "O slow to believe! Ye of little faith!
Do you not understand yet? Have I been with
you so long, and you do not know who I am?"
Still, when He entered Olivet to pray, He wanted
their companionship: He wanted friends who
would pray with Him. And when they fell asleep,
God sent His Son an angel to refresh Him in His
agony.

When I have no one to comfort me in my
troubles, I must pray. God's grace will be my
angel.

II. THE SCOURGING AT THE PILLAR

"Ha! What have you to do with us, Jesus of Nazareth? Have you come to destroy us?"

Luke 4:34

EVIL is not comfortable in the presence of God. Jesus' enemies were not comfortable in His company. Judas was glad to be out of the supper room. Annas, unsettled by Christ's calm dignity amidst insults, quickly sent Him away. The Sanhedrin passed Him on to Pilate. Pilate, afraid to condemn a Man so manifestly more innocent than His judges, was much relieved to learn that Jesus was a Galilean. He ordered Him off to Herod. Herod soon tired of Him, and sent Him back. Then the bitter climax – the crowds yelled for His death, preferring the company of Barabbas.

Deserted by the friends He loved, shunned by His enemies (whom He also loved), Jesus bore His loneliness in silent patience. Would I?

III. THE CROWNING WITH THORNS

"Love is patient, love is kind."

1 Corinthians 13:4

LOVE was the whole reason for the Incarnation. Christ's life was one of loving service – healing, teaching, preaching to the poor. He called Himself the Good Shepherd, who would die for His sheep. He would have gathered His enemies to His heart as a hen gathers her chicks under her wings. He is as close to His friends as a vine to its branches. When He was about to leave the world, His love found a way to remain – hidden under the appearances of bread and wine. But on Good Friday, when Pilate pointed Him out to the crowd, they forgot His goodness. The sheep demanded the death of the Good Shepherd.

Alone, forsaken, blasphemed, Jesus kept loving. If His people would kill Him, He would die for them. A lesson for me about how God defines love.

IV. THE CARRYING OF THE CROSS

"Large numbers of people followed Him, and of women too, who mourned and lamented for Him."

Luke 23:27

NOBLE-HEARTED women are found on nearly every page of the Gospel. There is, of course, the incomparable Mother of God, Mary. There is the old Elizabeth, the ancient Anna, and the young Magdalen, "who loved greatly"; the Canaanite woman who begged like a dog for Christ's help; the woman whose touch drew healing power from Jesus; the widow whose farthing enriched God's house "above gold and precious stone"; and Pilate's wife, Our Lord's only defender in His Passion. And there were the women who made the Way of the Cross with Him to comfort His heart with their tears.

To console others, to relieve their loneliness with our sympathy, is a great virtue. "Blessed are they that mourn."

V. THE CRUCIFIXION

"My God, My God, why hast Thou forsaken Me?"
                                    Matthew 27:46

IT was inevitable that our Lord's friends should not understand Him. He was a perfect Man among proud, unspiritual men; and He was God, whose ways are not ours. Even His Mother didn't always understand His words and actions and had to puzzle over them in her heart. His heavenly Father alone understood Jesus Christ completely. Our Lord's chief delight was to spend His nights in prayerful intimacy with His Father, away from the shallow squabbling of His disciples. On Calvary, however, Jesus felt abandoned.

If Jesus could feel abandoned by His Father, so can I. And if Jesus could continue to pray, so can I.

The Glorious Mysteries

The Resurrection
The Ascension of our Lord
The Descent of the Holy Spirit
The Assumption of our Lady
   into Heaven
The Coronation of the Blessed
   Virgin Mary

THE GLORIES OF MARY

Our Lady will give us a deeper understanding
of the *glories of Mary* through the five Glorious
Mysteries

—one—
Our Father, Who art in Heaven...
—ten—
Hail Mary, full of grace...
—one—
Glory be to the Father...

I. THE RESURRECTION

"... For the Almighty has done great things for me."
                                            Luke 1:49

MARY, it's much easier to talk to you than about you. At first sight, it might seem otherwise because you are not just anyone; you are God's mother. *Mother of God, Mother of God...* I like to let these words run through my mind. The more I think about God, how good He is, how kind and loving – eternal, infinite – God, who made me and everything else (yes, and you, Mary) out of nothing – the better I understand your dignity. If it is wonderful "that we should be called and should be the children of God," how much more wonderful that you should be called, and should be, God's Mother!

Mary, I thank God for you every day of my life. And I thank you for God, come to earth by your "Fiat."

II. THE ASCENSION OF OUR LORD

"The faithful all lived together and owned everything in common; they sold their goods and possessions and shared out the proceeds among themselves according to what each one needed."

Acts 2:44-45

DURING your life, Mary, you hated one thing – sin. You knew how much it offends God; you stood by while sin drove nails through your Son's hands and feet. You saw the malice of sin perfectly, although you never offended God in the slightest way. And I! When I look at a crucifix I see the effect of sin, but I don't understand as I should. How different, you and I! I thank God, Mary, that by your Immaculate Conception you were kept free from the slightest trace of sin.

Mary, obtain for me a grace you had no need of – the grace to resist my own selfishness.

III. THE DESCENT OF THE HOLY SPIRIT

"Hail, favored one! The Lord is with you."

Luke 1:28

STILL another privilege of yours, Mary, makes me feel very little beside you. I reflect how often I've refused to follow the invitations of God's grace; how often, perhaps, I've even fallen from the state of grace, living to repent only by God's sheerest mercy. Then I remember how different you were – full of grace! Full of grace at your Immaculate Conception; filled with a new fullness at the Incarnation, at the Nativity, on Calvary, at Pentecost, at your death; and at every moment of your life, growing beyond belief in the loving friendship of God.

Hail Mary, full of grace! Pray for us sinners.

IV. THE ASSUMPTION OF OUR LADY INTO HEAVEN

"Jesus, the only mediator, is the way of our prayer; Mary, his mother and ours, is wholly transparent to him."
                                        Catechism, no. 2674

I was born a human, Mary; you were conceived Immaculate. Like you, I am an adopted child of God, but you are His Mother as well. As a human being I sin. Your crucified Son redeemed me. Still I don't understand humility. By the very fact that I was born, I am sentenced to die; and when my soul departed to its place in eternity, my body will return to dust. But when you died, Mary, God blessed you for your perfect life. You were able to join your Son in heaven.

May God be blessed forever, Mary, for your goodness. And may I be with you forever to bless God.

V. THE CORONATION OF THE BLESSED VIRGIN MARY

"Mary 'aided the beginning of the Church by her prayers ... we also see Mary by her prayers imploring the gift of the Spirit.'"   *Catechism, no. 965*

MARY, in these meditations I have been thinking of all the things that set you in a place apart among all the creatures of God's hand. The Blessed Trinity, Jesus – you bow your head before Them; and they raise you high above all the rest of creation, "as a mountain set upon mountains." It could make me feel insignificant, very little, helpless – but I am not discouraged. Because "little and helpless" is almost the definition of a child – and I am your child, Mary. You are my Mother. The more God exalts you by His grace, and the more lofty your queenly throne in heaven, the more quickly do I run to you, as a child of God's Mother should.

"I will not leave you orphans." "Behold Your Mother."

Personal Notes

The
Joyful
Mysteries

The Annunciation
The Visitation
The Birth of our Lord
The Presentation in the Temple
The Finding of the Child Jesus in
the Temple

SIN

Our Lady will give us a deeper understanding of
sin through the five Joyful Mysteries

—one—
Our Father, Who art in Heaven...
—ten—
Hail Mary, full of grace...
—one—
Glory be to the Father...

173

I. THE ANNUNCIATION

"He was bearing our faults in His own body on the cross, so that we might die to our faults and live for holiness; through His wounds you have been healed."
1 Peter 2:24-25

WHAT delicacy on the part of God is Gabriel's message to Mary! This was the first day of the world's "second Spring." Gabriel's "greeting of the season" brought unalloyed joy to Mary: "Full of grace! Mother of God by God's overshadowing! The Son of the Most High is come! David's Lord, King of the world without end!" The birth of Jesus – the Alpha and Omega of redemption. But not a syllable was uttered about that grim, gray thing – the crucifying of the Good-man – Salvation from all sin through the cross.

Savior – Gabriel did not mention that! But Jesus became incarnate to undo the world's sins and to help me repent of mine.

II. THE VISITATION

"For at the moment the sound of your greeting reached my ears, the infant in my womb leaped for joy."

Luke 1:44

THE mysteries of the divine babyhood are rightly called joyful. Adam's sin had begotten our weakness; weakness and pride sired worldwide sin; from personal sin came the world's collective gloom. Hope held one pinched foot at the threshold of heaven – God had promised a Savior. God would act in Jesus. God would reawaken in us our absolute dependence on Him. God would accept us as sinners and love us anyway. How great is the mercy of God!

Mary teach me to leap for joy as John did in the womb of his mother Elizabeth. Jesus came to bring abundant life. Alleluia!

175

III. THE BIRTH OF OUR LORD

"For today in the city of David a Savior has been born for you who is Messiah and Lord."

Luke 2:11

JESUS was going to win pardon from the world in a very remarkable way. Those He came to save would turn upon Him. Their hatred would crucify Him. Then it was done – the world was saved. He could have saved the world in any other way. But no, there should be no redemption until we had rejected the Redeemer. Of this, the manner of His birth was a quiet prophecy. He must be born at Bethlehem; yet in Bethlehem there was no room; and He was born, as He would die, "outside the walls", where Bethlehem's shepherd found Him.

Jesus had been rejected enough. I should reject sin by keeping away from temptation.

IV. THE PRESENTATION IN THE TEMPLE

"And a sword will pierce your own soul, too ..."

Luke 2:35

FORTY days after the birth of Jesus, Mary and Joseph presented Jesus to His Father in the Temple. Joseph gave the priest two turtledoves, and Jesus was brought back – "redeemed." It was a striking preparation for what was to follow; this was the day of two redemptions: one of fulfillment and one of prophecy. The Holy Family approached the Temple gate. An old man stopped them and asked for the Child, then filled their ears with prophecy. This Child would redeem the world, but not by offering turtledoves. He was set for contradiction, and Mary was set for a sword.

Sin put a lance through the side of Jesus, and a sword through Mary's soul. At Fatima Mary asked for my daily Rosary in reparation for sin.

V. THE FINDING OF THE CHILD JESUS IN THE TEMPLE

"Your father and I have been looking for you with great anxiety."

Luke 2:48

SIN causes deep discontent of the soul – always. We cannot tell ourselves otherwise. But not all sorrow comes from personal sin. Trials are not always punishments; Mary's certainly was not. Inner conflict does not always signify estrangement from God; Mary never offended Him. Mary's faith, her love for God, fed upon sorrow; she pleased God as much in her three-day agony as she had in her joy at His birth.

To give up, to lose confidence in God when things go wrong – what a temptation! Mary didn't. I shouldn't.

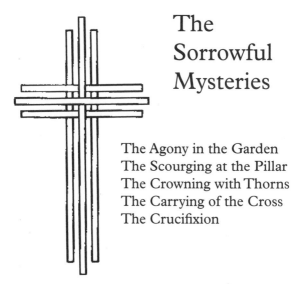

The Sorrowful Mysteries

The Agony in the Garden
The Scourging at the Pillar
The Crowning with Thorns
The Carrying of the Cross
The Crucifixion

PILATE

Our Lady will give us a deeper understanding of
Pilate through the five Sorrowful Mysteries

—one—
Our Father, Who art in Heaven...
—ten—
Hail Mary, full of grace...
—one—
Glory be to the Father...

I. THE AGONY IN THE GARDEN

"Have nothing to do with that righteous man."
Matthew 27:19

WHILE Jesus was in torment in Gethsemane, Pilate's wife asleep in her palace had a dream. She saw Jesus, and learned that He was altogether sinless; and she saw herself suffering much on account of Him. Claudia Procla spent a restless morning; her anxiety became acute when she heard that Jesus of Nazareth was on trial for His life before her husband. She sent a message to Pilate immediately: "This Man is innocent; let Him be."

Pilate knew Christ was guiltless, and his wife's remarkable message proved it. Even so, he crucified Christ. I also have the power to oppose the grace of God. I should pray every day for the grace not to resist grace.

II. THE SCOURGING AT THE PILLAR

"Then Pilate took Jesus and had Him scourged."

John 19:1

PILATE was disturbed by the meek majesty of his prisoner. He turned abruptly and disappeared into his palace, then had Jesus brought before him – to remind Christ that He was only a prisoner, nothing more. "What is your crime?" asked Pilate, hiding his interest beneath a mask of official boredom. Jesus replied, "My Kingdom is not of this world." That was indeed His crime in the eyes of His accusers; their kingdom was very much of this world. Pilate knew that Jesus was no criminal; but Pilate was a worldling, like the Pharisees, so he sent Jesus to be scourged.

God so loved the world as to die for it. Pilate so loved the world as to crucify Christ. Do I love the world as Christ did – or as Pilate loved it?

III. THE CROWNING WITH THORNS

"All things came to be through him, and without him nothing came to be."   *John 1:3*

ON Christ's own testimony, Pilate sinned less than Caiphas and the Pharisees. "The one who delivered Me to you has the greater sin." The Pharisees had seen Jesus heal on the Sabbath; saw Him dispossess devils with a word; stood by the tomb as Lazarus came forth; heard Christ preach the kingdom of God, His own Kingdom; then with superb malice they plotted His death. Pilate spoke with Jesus for just a few minutes; saw no miracles; knew nothing of His teaching. But Pilate did know that Jesus was a King; and part of his sin was to allow the Savior's bloody coronation.

Pilate sinned through cowardice, not through malice. But he sinned. Fortitude to resist temptation is a gift of God, mine for asking.

IV. THE CARRYING OF THE CROSS

"Like a sheep he was led to the slaughter, and as a lamb before its shearer is silent, so he opened not his mouth."

Acts 8:32

GOD is no respecter of position, but we are. When the Magi spoke of the Savior's birth – "all Jerusalem was troubled" – but only because Herod was troubled. And another Herod had not wanted to kill John the Baptist; he consented only "out of respect for his guests." The whole purpose of life, thought the Pharisees, was to impress people with a show of piety. Human respect led Peter to deny Christ. And human respect led Pilate to condemn Him to death. When the crowd shouted, "If you free Him, you're no friend of Caesar." Pilate's resistance gave way, and he left Jesus to their mercy.

Human respect – fearing what others will think about our actions – often generates sin, and robs even virtue of its merit. Do I act to please God – or others?

V. THE CRUCIFIXION

"Pilate had an inscription written and put on the cross."   *John 19:19*

THE soldiers, followed by the crowd, led Jesus away to Calvary. Pilate was alone in the palace, intensely angry with himself and with the Pharisees. He played the coward; and far worse, he realized that the Jews had used his cowardice to gain their purpose – the death of Jesus. Pilate had retaliated, as cowards will; he had a placard nailed to the top of the cross, "Jesus of Nazareth, King of the Jews." The Pharisees were indignant, but Pilate stood his ground. "What I have written, I have written."

There was much of the Pharisee in Pilate. He gave in on the great issue, Christ's death; but he was adamant in the petty wrangle about the placard. Do I fuss over trifles, and neglect things vital to my soul?

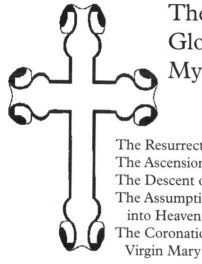

The Glorious Mysteries

The Resurrection
The Ascension of our Lord
The Descent of the Holy Spirit
The Assumption of our Lady
   into Heaven
The Coronation of the Blessed
   Virgin Mary

MARY AND JESUS

Our Lady will give us a deeper understanding of
Mary and Jesus through the five Glorious Mysteries

—one—
Our Father, Who art in Heaven...
—ten—
Hail Mary, full of grace...
—one—
Glory be to the Father...

185

I. THE RESURRECTION

"Do not fear, Mary, for you have found favor with God."   *Luke 1:30*

"GOD'S ways are beyond us." I think of that, Mary, when I meditate upon the Annunciation scene. The desires of your pure heart were inconceivably grand; you longed for the Messiah with an intensity that awed the Seraphim; still even you, Mary, never suspected what was in God's mind. You dreamt of being the Savior's servant. God wanted you to be the Mother of His Son. You consented to be His Mother as you proclaimed yourself His servant. "Behold the handmaid of the Lord." At that moment you conceived Jesus through the power of the Holy Spirit. Jesus, whose heavenly life began in a tomb, began His earthly life in your womb.

Hail, Mary! Blessed is the Fruit of thy womb, Jesus!

II. THE ASCENSION OF OUR LORD

"Then he led them out as far as Bethany, raised his hands, and blessed them."   *Luke 24:50*

YOU must have been on Olivet with the Apostles, Mary, when your Son blessed them and rose out of sight. And it must have been you who caught the last loving glance from His eyes. Perhaps the white cloud that gathered about His glorious body reminded you of the swaddling-clothes you wrapped the Infant Jesus in. Perhaps, beholding Him for the last time on earth, you remembered the first time you saw Him, the divine Babe-in-arms. When the newborn Christ offered Himself to His Father – "I have come to do Thy will, O God!" – He did so in the chalice of your arms.

You saw Jesus first, Mary, and you saw Him last. Grant that I may see Him forever.

III. THE DESCENT OF THE HOLY SPIRIT

"The Lord may grant you times of refreshment"

Acts 3:20

ON Pentecost, Mary, the Holy Spirit descended upon you – for the second time. The first time, many years before in your home in Nazareth, He fashioned Jesus in your virginal body. What was His gift to you on Pentecost? I think the spirit's gift must have been very much like the first gift to you. The Holy Spirit is "the Spirit of Jesus." On Pentecost, you loved and understood Jesus as you never had loved Him before.

The Holy Spirit lives in my soul helping me to love and understand Christ. Help me remember God's real presence in my heart.

IV. THE ASSUMPTION OF OUR LADY INTO HEAVEN

"Those who die in God's grace and friendship and are perfectly purified live forever with Christ."

Catechism, no. 1023

A very holy woman, to whom Jesus had often appeared, once said: "Me liked no other Heaven than Jesus." That artless medieval expression is an echo of the single thought that must have filled your heart, Mary, as you rose up to heaven. "I am going to Jesus who is my heaven!" Jesus was everything to you. If anyone had asked you – "Why did God make you?" – you would have answered, "For Jesus." Your soul was a compass needle that pointed only to your Son. And when you went to heaven, you might have spoken to Jesus the words He once addressed to the Father: "now glorify Me with Thyself."

Mary loved Jesus and did everything for God. When that can be said for me, I will be ready for heaven.

V. THE CORONATION OF THE BLESSED VIRGIN MARY

"The 'splendor of an entirely unique holiness' by which Mary is 'enriched from the first instant of her conception' comes wholly from Christ."

Catechism, no. 492

I have been meditating, Mary, on the joy that filled your heart as you soared toward Jesus. But your happiness in being with Him once again, and forever, met more than its match in the delight that filled the Sacred Heart of your Son. Yours was the vast heart of a Mother; His was the Heart of God. Your divine Son "had possessed you from the beginning of His life on earth." He would exhaust His greatness in devising privileges for His mother. Long before you were crowned Queen of Heaven, you were made Queen-Mother of the Prince of Peace.

You are Queen in heaven, Mary, because you had been a queen on earth.

Personal Notes

The Joyful Mysteries

The Annunciation
The Visitation
The Birth of our Lord
The Presentation in the Temple
The Finding of the Child Jesus
   in the Temple

CHASTITY

Our Lady will give us a deeper understanding of
chastity through the five Joyful Mysteries

—one—
Our Father, Who art in Heaven...
—ten—
Hail Mary, full of grace...
—one—
Glory be to the Father...

193

I. THE ANNUNCIATION

"How can this be, since I have no relations with a man?"
Luke 1:34

MARY'S "angelic purity" – that poetic phrase is a misfortune. It makes Mary a little unapproachable. It tries to say Mary was chaste. Chastity is a human virtue, and Mary's was perfect because of grace. It was grace that kept her soul free from original sin; grace, too, that led her to vow her virginity to God. Mary was a virgin; Mary was pure, by grace.

I need grace to be chaste. The will to be chaste is necessary as well, but it is not enough. I must understand that or I shall not be chaste. And I must pray for that grace daily.

II. THE VISITATION

"The light shines in the darkness, and the darkness has not overcome it." John 1:5

ORIGINAL sin did not change our nature, but it did weaken it. God had made us as He had made everything else, in an orderly way – mind over matter. Adam and Eve's pride introduced a spirit of selfishness into our lower faculties and passions. Now our "matter" wants satisfaction that doesn't always lead us to God. We need help to find our way. Mary brought this help to Elizabeth's home; it was her Son.

The grace I need to be pure – I owe to Jesus Christ. The more I feel my weakness and ask His aid, the more He is ready to help me. Mary pray with me.

III. THE BIRTH OF OUR LORD

"She gave birth to her firstborn son."

Luke 2:7

CHRISTMAS was the beginning of the new creation. The Church, to all appearances a mere organization, is really an organism – the Mystical Body of Christ, a Body living and breathing the life of God by grace. We are the cells of this Body. We are meant to grow to "the fullness of Christ." That is why Jesus, the head of the Mystical Body, did not come to earth full-grown out of the clouds, but was born a Child.

Jesus being born of a woman brings having children to a new level of holiness. Mary be with all who are about to give birth.

IV. THE PRESENTATION IN THE TEMPLE

"But the days will come when the bridegroom is taken away from them, and then they will fast on that day."
Mark 2:20

ANNA'S life story is startling, but the point of it is practical and commonplace. Self-discipline of soul and body is good for us. Anna's coming to live in the Temple as a young woman was self-discipline. Fasting kept her body quiet, leaving her free for constant prayer to God. The resulting spotlessness of heart and mind and body enabled her to see the Savior in a Child. "Blessed are the clean of heart, for they shall see God."

My vocation is not Anna's, but self-discipline of mind and body ought to be. Avoiding unnecessary temptations and moderation in all things –good rules to live by!

V. FINDING OF THE CHILD JESUS IN THE TEMPLE

"You are lacking in one thing. Go sell what you have, and give to the poor and you will have treasure in heaven; then come, follow me."

Mark 10:21

ALMOST thirty of our Lord's thirty-three years on earth were passed at out-of-the-way Nazareth in a sort of rural oblivion. Jesus lived an obscure life of which we know nothing, except that He grew in grace and wisdom. His mind was not idle, nor His heart; they were altogether preoccupied with "His Father's business." Only once did He give expression to His intense activity of soul, when, as a boy of twelve, He left Mary and Joseph to instruct the teachers of the law. It is our one glimpse into a heart eaten up with zeal for the Father's house.

I want to have that zeal for God. Mary lead me to the people, places and things that will help me develop an intense love of God.

The Sorrowful Mysteries

The Agony in the Garden
The Scourging at the Pillar
The Crowning with Thorns
The Carrying of the Cross
The Crucifixion

THE POOR

Our Lady will give us a deeper understanding of *the poor* through the five Sorrowful Mysteries

—one—
Our Father, Who art in Heaven...
—ten—
Hail Mary, full of grace...
—one—
Glory be to the Father...

199

I. THE AGONY IN THE GARDEN

"Blessed are the poor in spirit for theirs is the kingdom of heaven."   *Matthew 5:3*

THE poor are a favorite theme with Jesus. "Do not lay treasures on earth," He said in His first sermon; "and the people heard Him gladly," because they were poor. He grieved openly over the rich young man, possessed by his possessions. He told the pointed tale of a fool who dreamed of bigger barns on his deathbed. He praised the widow who put her last penny into the Temple treasury. And what He preached, Jesus practiced. The night before He died, He renounced an army of glorious angels, His possession by right, and entered upon His Passion (as He had entered the world) poor in spirit.

In these meditations, dear Lord, help me to understand what I can do to help the poor in spirit.

II. THE SCOURGING AT THE PILLAR

"Do not store up for yourselves treasures on earth, where moth and decay destroy."   *Matthew 6:19*

JESUS was a poor Man, but He did not despise men of wealth. As a Baby, He had received gifts of gold from the Magi. He befriended money-changers; one of them became an Apostle. "He looked upon the rich young man and loved him." He dined with the well-to-do, with Simon the Pharisee, with Zacheus. A rich man, Joseph of Arimathea, was to have the privilege of burying Him. Clearly, the sun of His divine love shone upon poor and rich alike. But He did warn rich men not to rest in their riches, if they wish to rest in Him. The Kingdom of Christ is "out of this world."

Jesus loved the rich young man in spite of his wealth; the rich young men left Jesus because of his wealth. Do I love the good life more than Jesus?

III. THE CROWNING WITH THORNS

"Jesus went around to all the towns and villages."
Matthew 9:35

JESUS lived in poverty, but never in squalor. By force of circumstance, He was born in a cave, but Mary wrapped Him in immaculate swaddling-bands, and laid Him on fresh, clean straw. Our Lord's home in Nazareth was an average dwelling. Jesus' plain rough robe did not embarrass Him in the presence of fashionable aristocracy. On the other hand, He avoided any affectation of elegance. "Don't fret about your clothing," He once said. Indeed, the only time He was royally dressed was in His Passion, when the jeering soldiers threw a scarlet cloak about His bleeding Body.

The spirit of simplicity avoids extremes. Jesus lived a simple life. Do I?

IV. THE CARRYING OF THE CROSS

"Do not weep for me; weep instead for yourselves and for your children." Luke 23:28

JESUS was a sorry sight as He dragged Himself along to Calvary. Here was a man who within a few hours had lost everything: friends, reputation, majestic bearing, commanding eloquence. His miraculous might had apparently become a mere memory. He is the divine poor man, whose only possession is a cross. But Jesus does not want sympathy. He accepts His lot, because it is the way to bring His Father completely into this world. He tells a group of mourning women to save their tears for themselves and their children; when Jerusalem is destroyed, many of them will grieve.

Our world is full of poor people on their way to Calvary. They need more than my sympathy. Especially, they need my prayers.

V. THE CRUCIFIXION

"But seek first the Kingdom of God."

Matthew 6:33

TWICE especially Jesus showed His great love for the poor: at His birth and at His death. A royal palace would not have been fine enough to welcome His august divinity. Instead, He chose to be born of poor parents outside the town of Bethlehem, in a stable. When He was dead, the world was saved and heaven opened, we might expect angelic splendor to shine about His body. Instead, He was buried as He had been born – outside the city in another man's cave.

When we die, we will bring before God only the wealth of our virtue. Am I rich in God's eyes?

The Glorious Mysteries

The Resurrection
The Ascension of our Lord
The Descent of the Holy Spirit
The Assumption of our Lady
  into Heaven
The Coronation of the Blessed
  Virgin Mary

MARY AND THE CHURCH

Our Lady will give us a deeper understanding of
Mary and the Church through the five Glorious
Mysteries

—one—
Our Father, Who art in Heaven...
—ten—
Hail Mary, full of grace...
—one—
Glory be to the Father...

I. THE RESURRECTION

"Serve with my spirit." Romans 1:9

UNTIL your Son's Resurrection, Mary, your part in the drama of Redemption was played behind a nearly closed curtain. Only a few people knew that God was your Son. During His public life, you crossed the stage only two or three times. You might have made the declaration of John the Baptist your own. "He must increase, I must decrease." On Calvary, to all appearances, you were only a Mother with a crushed heart watching her condemned Son die. But after the Apostles had seen the risen Lord, they gravitated toward you, His Mother.

My part in God's drama may appear insignificant. But a saint who plays a small part well – as Mary did, can "save the play."

II. THE ASCENSION OF OUR LORD

*"Coming in from Olivet, they all gave themselves up
to prayer, with Mary the Mother of Jesus."*

Acts 1:14

THE ten days between the Lord's Ascension and
Pentecost would have been awkward ones for the
Apostles – if you hadn't been with them, Mary.
To be sure, they were not numb with utter disillu-
sionment as they had been between Good Friday
and Easter. On the contrary, they radiated joyous
expectancy. Still, they were not yet "clothed with
the power from on high," not yet confirmed in
grace by the mighty wind and tiny flame of Pentecost, the "sacraments" of the Holy Spirit. They
were still very emotional, excitable, impetuous
– and they needed the gentle, untroubled, loving
presence of a mother.

The spirit that leads me is not always God's. If
Apostles needed Mary, how much more do I?

III. THE DESCENT OF THE HOLY SPIRIT

"They were all filled with the Holy Spirit."

Acts 2:4

FOR the Apostles, the citizenry, the pilgrims to the Holy City "from every country under heaven," Pentecost was certainly a remarkable day. Says the author of The Acts of the Apostles: "The crowds are bewildered, beside themselves with astonishment," as the Apostles began to preach Christ in every known language. The Holy Spirit had given them that marvelous gift among many others. What gifts did He give you, Mary? Not only to speak many tongues, but to listen to many hearts. You were able to be everyone's Mother, Mary. All Christians were to run to you with their worries and troubles. Simeon had prophesied this of you: "the secret thoughts of many will be laid bare."

Mary, can I tell you my secret thoughts?

IV. THE ASSUMPTION OF OUR LADY INTO HEAVEN

"Taken up to heaven she did not lay aside this saving office but by her intercession continues to bring us the gifts of eternal salvation."

Lumen Gentium para. 62

"IT is expedient for you that I go," Jesus had said to His downcast Apostles. It was God's plan that the Holy Spirit, the Spirit of loving zeal and true holiness, should not descend until Jesus had ascended. You, Mary, might have said the same thing to the Apostles as they gathered about you just before your death. It is expedient for you that I go. Just as my Son is closer to you in heaven than He ever was on earth, so shall I be. Every grace of Jesus can come through the communion of saints.

Mary, you are a saint and my mother. Help me pray my Rosary every day.

V. THE CORONATION OF THE BLESSED VIRGIN MARY

"The Blessed Virgin is invoked in the Church under the title Advocate . . ."

Catechism, no. 969

ON earth, Mary, you were mother – infinitely tender, understanding, compassionate. In heaven, while you are our Mother still, you are much more. When the Church sings of you: "Fair art thou daughter of Jerusalem," she adds this thunderous refrain: " – and terrible as an army set for the fray!" The gentle, humble Mother of Jesus, sword in hand! What do you make war upon, Mary? The Church tells me: "Rejoice, Mary, Virgin! Thou alone hast destroyed all the world's heresies!" It is against sin and unbelief that Mary leads the army of God.

Mary is meek, but Mary is mighty. Sin is confounded in the beads of her Rosary.

211

Personal Notes

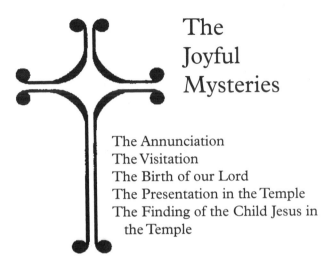

The Joyful Mysteries

The Annunciation
The Visitation
The Birth of our Lord
The Presentation in the Temple
The Finding of the Child Jesus in
    the Temple

SAINT JOSEPH

Our Lady will give us a deeper understanding of
Saint Joseph through the five Joyful Mysteries

—one—
Our Father, Who art in Heaven...
—ten—
Hail Mary, full of grace...
—one—
Glory be to the Father...

I. THE ANNUNCIATION

"Mary was betrothed to Joseph; but before they came to live together she was found to be with child through the Holy Spirit."　　　　*Matthew 1:18*

GREAT gladness for Mary! God's own doing, the Son of God growing in her womb. Joyful Mysteries indeed for her, but for Joseph, sad bewilderment. He knew nothing of the angel's visitation, nothing of God's overshadowing. He knew only of Mary's sanctity and still read the peace of innocence in her eyes; yet she was with child. Joseph could say nothing. He could only endure a storm of perplexities, until an angel dispersed the clouds: "Do not be afraid to take Mary home as your wife, she has conceived by the Holy Spirit."

Joseph bore his trial, the Cross of the Christ Child, in silent, trustful patience. His silence says to me: Do likewise.

II. THE VISITATION

"Mary remained with her about three months."

Luke 1:56

IN quick response to the angel's revelation, Mary hastened to the home of her cousin Elizabeth. In Nazareth, Joseph was left alone to his thoughts. He reflected on this beautiful woman who was so blessed by God. His love for her was a holy thing; it was that highest form of love, the silent gazing on the spiritual. That is why, in the Gospels, Joseph has nothing to say. Mary was his joyful mystery.

I am often lost in my thoughts. Do I love as Joseph did?

III. THE BIRTH OF OUR LORD

"Joseph... of the house and family of David."
                                    Matthew 1:20

TWENTY-EIGHT generations had seen the descendants of David brought to humble station. David had been heir to the splendid spoils of a hundred petty kingdoms; King Solomon, his son, bowed low to no man on earth; but Joseph of Nazareth was a carpenter. Still the vocation is not the man. King David's penitential psalmody was no fictional piety – adultery and murder were his crimes; Solomon, maker of God's Temple, worshipped idols and did not repent, whereas Joseph of Nazareth was a most holy man. His was the regal soul: a fit court, even in a cave, for the tiny Prince of Peace who saw only with the eyes of God.

St. Joseph's was not "headline" holiness. He is patron of unnoticed saints. He'd like to be mine!

IV. THE PRESENTATION IN THE TEMPLE

"Whoever enters through me will be saved, and will come in and go out and find pasture."

John 10:9

THE doorway to sanctity has a double lock. Doing one's duty is the outside key. Joseph was meticulous about this. Simply, he "fulfilled all thing prescribed." But so did the Pharisees. They spent their lives doing just the right thing. They could match Joseph in this. But they had only the outside key, and theirs was "outside" piety. Joseph had the inside key, doing one's duty for God: praying, working, sleeping, eating, all to please God, who sees what we do in secret.

It takes only a moment to say, "For You, Lord," as I begin my day, and each activity of the day becomes a prayer and the inside key.

V. THE FINDING OF THE CHILD JESUS IN THE TEMPLE

"Faith is the realization of what is hoped for and evidence of things not seen."　　　　*Hebrews 11:1*

JOSEPH would not live to see Jesus die. But he was not spared the lot of the saints – suffering with Christ. To Joseph, the Incarnation had been an agonizing dilemma; for the Savior's birth, he could do no better than a cave. Herod's wrath had driven him to Egypt, there to fend for his family. He had stood by, heart heavy as stone, while Simeon somberly prophesied concerning Jesus and Mary. Now, his fifth and most terrible sorrow: he had lost the boy Jesus. Joseph, silent prophet of the Sorrowful Mysteries!

St. Joseph was a very human person. And so he suffered. He suffered as he did everything else – for God. It was part of his "inside key" – and is part of mine.

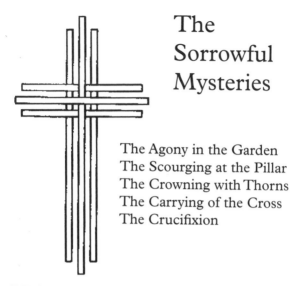

The Sorrowful Mysteries

The Agony in the Garden
The Scourging at the Pillar
The Crowning with Thorns
The Carrying of the Cross
The Crucifixion

DEATH

Our Lady will give us a deeper understanding of *death* through the five Sorrowful Mysteries

—one—
Our Father, Who art in Heaven...
—ten—
Hail Mary, full of grace...
—one—
Glory be to the Father...

219

I. THE AGONY IN THE GARDEN

"My soul is sorrowful even to death."

Matthew 26:38

JESUS Christ was a supreme idealist. He expressed His great ambition at the Last Supper: "Father keep those you have given Me true to Your Name so that they may be one like Us." But Jesus was a realist as well. He knew the price He had to pay for His divine idealism. "The Son of Man will be delivered into the power of men; they will put Him to death." Jesus had to suffer and die. And in the Garden of Olives, His soul seemed to dissolve at the thought of His coming Passion.

Christianity does not do away with death. But it does give death its meaning. Our faith is the only thing that gives suffering and death meaning. Thank you Jesus.

II. THE SCOURGING AT THE PILLAR

"We do not have the right to execute anyone."

John 18:31

NOTHING was more attractive in the personality of Christ than His spirit of optimism. To the Jews of Palestine, a proud people subject to Rome, spirituality starved by the laws of the Pharisees and Scribes, the Savior's heartening words were like the first delightful breath of spring after a long winter. The essence of His message was confidence in God, the Father, who watches over His children, knowing all their needs. God knew the suffering of the children of Israel. God loved them and knew only Jesus could make a difference.

God did not take pleasure in the suffering of His children or in the death of His Son. If suffering can be a blessing, surely death can be. God has blessed both by sending Jesus to us.

III. THE CROWNING WITH THORNS

"Behold your King! Crucify Him!"

John 19:14-15

JESUS Christ was only thirty-three when He died. Some people, failing to understand the meaning of Our Lord's life, regret His "untimely death." "How sad," they say; "undone at such an age! His best years still before Him! Think of the miracles He might have wrought, the wise words He would have spoken! In a few more years the Pharisees themselves would have fallen to their knees before Him!"

Jesus' life and death were complete. He did not need to do or say any more. We simply need to believe.

God help me understand the message of your Son's life and death. Help me be your witness here on earth.

IV. THE CARRYING OF THE CROSS

"A large crowd of people followed Jesus, including many women who mourned and lamented him."

Luke 23:27

SIMON was glad after a while to help Christ with His cross; the holy women wept as He passed by; Veronica wiped His face with her veil. But Mary just looked at her Son: her Child, her Baby. Mary and Jesus looked at each other. The heart of God, the heart of God's Mother, loving each other with immense love. Such love, such sorrow – each completely crushed at the other's immense sorrow.

God wants me to accept not only my own death, but also, the passing of those I love, when God calls them. Like Mary, I'll grieve; like Mary, I must trust in God.

V. THE CRUCIFIXION

"And we saw his glory, the glory as of the Father's only Son."   *John 1:14*

DYING had not been an easy matter for Jesus. But being dead was glorious. The world was redeemed, though it did not yet know it. All creation had become the chosen race. After His death, Jesus hastened to the right hand of the Father bringing with Him the soul of the good thief. All the bitter suffering He had borne for the world was a thing of the past. Glory, honor, power, exaltation and endless bliss awaited Him in His Father's house where He reigns forever.

Death is not the end of life. It is only after death that I will really begin to live.

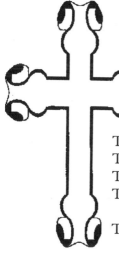

The Glorious Mysteries

The Resurrection
The Ascension of our Lord
The Descent of the Holy Spirit
The Assumption of our Lady
 into Heaven
The Coronation of the Blessed
 Virgin Mary

MARY AND MYSELF

Our Lady will give us a deeper understanding of
Mary and myself through the five Glorious
Mysteries

—one—
Our Father, Who art in Heaven...
—ten—
Hail Mary, full of grace...
—one—
Glory be to the Father...

225

I. THE RESURRECTION

"They devoted themselves to the teaching of the Apostles and to the communal life, to the breaking of the bread."   *Acts 2:42*

MEDITATING upon your life, Mary, fills me with deepest admiration. But you care very little about that. Admiration is an easy virtue. You want more than awe; you want imitation. You want me to love your Son as you loved Him; to love my family and relatives as you loved Joseph and Elizabeth; to love my friends as you loved your neighbors in Nazareth; to love and pray for my enemies as you prayed for those who crucified your Son.

Mary help me to imitate your love – to imitate Christ.

II. THE ASCENSION OF OUR LORD

"Do not conform yourself to this age but be transformed, that you may discern the will of God, what is good and pleasing and perfect."   *Romans 12:2*

WHEN you appear in the Gospels, Mary, you avoid extremes. If asked to be God's Mother, another girl might have pleaded her unworthiness, or become self-complacent; but your consent came from your humility. Of course, you went "hastily" to Elizabeth; but then, charity requires no delay! At Cana, where Jesus seemed to refuse your request, you neither lost confidence nor got angry with Him; instead you quietly told the waiters, "Do as He tells you." On Calvary, you weren't overcome by grief or anger; you stood by your Son. And when He ascended to heaven, you neither tried to delay Him, nor mourned His going; you returned to Jerusalem to pray.

Mary, teach me the virtue of avoiding extremes in my conduct.

III. THE DESCENT OF THE HOLY SPIRIT

"Peace be with you."   *Luke 24:36*

THE Apostles were blessed on Pentecost; and perhaps the most remarkable grace was their new-born desire to suffer for Christ. Not merely the resigned acceptance of suffering, but joy of heart in the midst of contempt and persecution. You did not need to receive that grace on Pentecost, Mary. It had been conceived in your heart long before, when Jesus was conceived in your womb. You knew the Old Testament prophecies. You knew the Messiah would one day suffer. You knew He would be disfigured so inhumanely He would no longer look like a man. But you also knew Jesus had said He would be safe, at the right hand of the Father who loved Him as only God can love.

Mary, help me to be patient and trust God.

IV. THE ASSUMPTION OF OUR LADY INTO HEAVEN

"The Virgin Mary cooperated through free faith and obedience in human salvation. She uttered her yes in the name of all human nature."

St. Thomas Aquinas

When you were assumed to heaven, Mary, two of your noblest virtues dissolved in the light of glory. Your faith melted into sight, hope blossomed into reality. While on earth, you lived the most perfect life of faith the world has ever known. Mere reason did not tell you that Jesus was God. You believed it; you took God's word for it. When you saw your Son dying on the cross, you did not see God being reconciled with the world. You believed it because Jesus had declared that, by His death, He would draw all things to Himself.

Mary, help me to live a "life of faith" – to believe and to act accordingly.

V. THE CORONATION OF THE BLESSED VIRGIN MARY

"Mary's function as a mother of men in no way obscures or diminishes this unique mediation of Christ, but rather shows its power."

Catechism, no. 970

MANY not understanding you, Mary, don't know how to love you. They think there should be no one between them and God. They don't realize that your sole interest lies in bringing us closer to God.

I love you because Jesus did – I love you because Jesus told us to behold our mother. I know you love me because Jesus told you to behold us. The rest is beyond my understanding.

Mary, come with me as I journey to the Father in the way your Son has taught me to travel. Guide me.

231

Personal Notes

The Joyful Mysteries

The Annunciation
The Visitation
The Birth of our Lord
The Presentation in the Temple
The Finding of the Child Jesus
  in the Temple

HUMILITY

Our Lady will give us a deeper understanding of
humility through the five Joyful Mysteries

—one—
Our Father, Who art in Heaven...
—ten—
Hail Mary, full of grace...
—one—
Glory be to the Father...

233

I. THE ANNUNCIATION

*"I urge you to live in a manner worthy of your call ...
with all humility and gentleness, with patience."*
                                                Ephesians 4:1-2

HUMILITY has a bad name. Many dismiss it as
a perpetual hanging of the head, but that is not
humility. The one who confesses he has no gifts
is not humble. Mary of Nazareth, who knew she
was a child of God, was humble. Mary's thoughts
were lofty, because her thoughts were true. She
knew that her goodness, her greatness, came
altogether from God, and she acted accordingly.
Humility means acting upon the truth about God
and ourselves. It is a proud man who hangs his
head; otherwise, he would see God above him and
never look down.

Humble Mary became God's Mother – the
world's greatest person. Something for me to
meditate upon!

II. THE VISITATION

"Doing nothing out of selfishness, rather humbly, regard others ... look out not for his own interests, but everyone for those of others."

Philippians 2:3-4

PRIDE would be proper if it were possible for the human being to do anything without God. But it is not. We are completely dependent on God. Humility is accepting that dependence and finding joy in the love of the God who does everything for us. A water faucet is useless if the reservoir is closed; so, too, we are helpless when we try to act independently of God. That is why, when Elizabeth cried out, "Blessed art thou among women," Mary added the balancing truth: "He who is mighty has done great things for me."

Mary was practical and realistic because she sincerely referred all her goodness to God. Her humility was, literally, "down to earth." And I ... ?

III. THE BIRTH OF OUR LORD

"Let us go to Bethlehem to see this thing that has taken place."

Luke 2:15

THE most popular religious paintings are of the newborn Christ Child in the arms of His Mother – a very awesome thing. God became man; born of a woman. In the Incarnation, God, while remaining God, became one of us. A very humbling thought. No wonder artists are drawn to depict the unimaginable event. God could so love the world, God would send His only Son to teach us how to know the Father. If God loves me that much, I must be a wonderful creation. If God believes I can come to know Him through His Son, so be it.

Mary, you came to know the Father through your Son. Teach me your humble ways.

IV. THE PRESENTATION IN THE TEMPLE

"For if anyone thinks they are something when they are nothing, they are deluding themselves."

Galatians 6:3

THE proud man stands upon a pillar but so does the humble. The proud person poised on the pillar of inordinate self-esteem; the humble upon Christ. Proud people will never climb down the pillar of self; egotism hugs the heights; they must be toppled off. And when they fall, they realize how shaky the ground under the pillar of pride. But humbled souls need not climb the pillar; Christ will lift them up. Christ was set for the fall; He is set for the rise as well.

When I am weak, God is strong.

V. THE FINDING OF THE CHILD JESUS IN THE TEMPLE

"Whoever humbles himself like this child is the greatest in the Kingdom of Heaven."

Matthew 18:4

THE Incarnation was a divine gift. God bowed the heavens and came down and was made to our image and likeness. Jesus Christ was humility. As God, He knew perfectly, "what was in man"; as man, He confessed what He knew of His humanity: "Of Myself, I can do nothing." Nothing rhetorical or exaggerated about it; simply, people can do nothing good of themselves alone. That is in the nature of things. And it demands our recognition of our dependence on God. And Jesus, who came not to destroy the law but to fulfill it, went down to Nazareth.

Am I humble? My recognition of my dependence on God is humility.

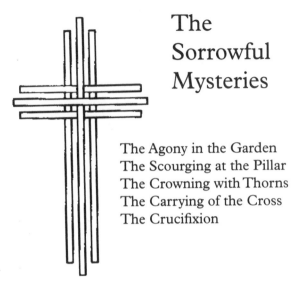

The Sorrowful Mysteries

The Agony in the Garden
The Scourging at the Pillar
The Crowning with Thorns
The Carrying of the Cross
The Crucifixion

PATIENCE

Our Lady will give us a deeper understanding of *patience* through the five Sorrowful Mysteries

—one—
Our Father, Who art in Heaven...
—ten—
Hail Mary, full of grace...
—one—
Glory be to the Father...

239

I. THE AGONY IN THE GARDEN

"Christ Jesus displayed all his patience as an example for those who would come to believe in him."

1 Timothy 1:16

JESUS once told the story of a poor man who owed his employer a large sum of money. "Be patient with me," he begged; and his master cancelled the debt. Jesus was that master, and the servant represented His disciples. Time after time Jesus asked more of His disciples than they were ready to give. He asked faith of Peter, and Peter sank beneath the waves; He asked humility of James and John, and they requested the first places in His Kingdom. And in the Garden, He asked His disciples to pray, and they slept. But Jesus was patient. He knew that, in time to come, they would understand.

Being patient can be painful. Do I give way to annoyance, exasperation, anger, when others fall short of my expectations?

II. THE SCOURGING AT THE PILLAR

*"We commend ourselves as ministers of God through
... patience and kindness in the power of God."*

2 Corinthians 6:6

THE Pharisees put Christ to the test. They led an
adulteress to Him to see if He would command
her to be stoned, and so appear heartless, or
demand her release and so break the Mosaic Law.
Instead, to the Pharisees' horror, He invites the
sinless ones among them to stone her, and they all
depart. To the Pharisees He said: "Render Caesar's things to Caesar, God's to God"; "straining
the gnat, you swallow the camel"; "the Sabbath
was made for man, not man for the Sabbath."
And the Gospel adds, "the Pharisees sat there in
silence." But in His Passion, while the Pharisees
calumniated Him, Jesus was silent.

Silence is the language of patience. Jesus was
silent in His sufferings because He saw God's will
in them. And I?

III. THE CROWNING WITH THORNS

"The God of Abraham, Isaac and Jacob has glorified his servant Jesus whom you handed over and denied in Pilate's presence."
                                                    Acts 3:13

THE crowd exulted when He raised a dead girl to life, but Jesus calmly ordered her to be fed. When the people hailed Him King, Jesus was especially unimpressed; once He hid on a mountain, and once He wept. He knew He was King, but a King in exile. "My Kingdom is not of this world." He knew He did not need to seek His own glory – He knew glory was given by the Father. And so, when His royalty was made sport of in His Passion, Jesus bore the humiliation patiently.

Jesus knew He was doing what was right and good. He was truthful, prayerful, and faithful. Those were His glories. And I ... ?

IV. THE CARRYING OF THE CROSS

"As they led Jesus away they took hold of a certain Simon."   Luke 23:26

IT had been a long, slow journey from his home in the country to Jerusalem, and Simon was tired at the end of it. Occupied with his own idle thoughts, he hardly noticed the stream of soldiers and citizens coming out through the city gate. But the soldiers noticed him. A moment later the astonished Simon found himself helping Jesus Christ carry His cross. Simon didn't like it at all, but he did as he was told; and it was not long before God enlightened his soul. Simon of Cyrene was the first to discover that the yoke of Christ is sweet, and His burden light.

When I am given difficult or thankless jobs, I must work at them patiently. "Come to me when you are weary."

V. THE CRUCIFIXION

"Father, into your hands I commend my spirit."

Luke 23:46

THESE words are the key to the incredible patience of Christ. For years He had allowed Himself to be imposed upon by others, to be misunderstood, misrepresented; He had worked a thousand miracles, but few gave Him thanks; His wonderful sermons, full of divine wisdom and love, often fell upon deaf ears; and at the end of a life of utter self-giving, He was betrayed, deserted, condemned to death and crucified. But it was not just His "bad luck"; it was His vocation. That is why Jesus was patient until His last breath. God entered totally into the suffering of the Christ.

"In patience you will possess your souls," Jesus once said. In His patience Christ possessed the souls of others. I can do the same, by uniting my silent endurance to His.

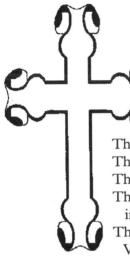

The Glorious Mysteries

The Resurrection
The Ascension of our Lord
The Descent of the Holy Spirit
The Assumption of our Lady
   into Heaven
The Coronation of the Blessed
   Virgin Mary

THE SECOND COMING OF CHRIST

Our Lady will give us a deeper understanding of
the second coming of Christ through the five Glorious
Mysteries

—one—
Our Father, Who art in Heaven...
—ten—
Hail Mary, full of grace...
—one—
Glory be to the Father...

245

I. THE RESURRECTION

"I pray not for them, but also for those who will be-
lieve in me through their word."

John 17:20

FOR many people, belief in the end of the world is a fairy-tale, or an escape mechanism born of chaotic world conditions. For a Christian, it is neither a myth nor a sedative. The world's collapse, and Christ's second coming, are as much a part of His faith as the world's creation and Christ's first coming at Nazareth. The glorified Savior who made the earth tremble at His Resurrection, will shake the heavens on the last day. He was born at Bethlehem humble and meek; in the last times He will appear as the God of power and love who fulfills the world.

I may not live to see the last day; still, Jesus will be my Lord. Am I ready for Christ's coming?

II. THE ASCENSION OF OUR LORD

"Therefore my heart has been glad and my tongue has exulted; my flesh, too, will dwell in hope."

Acts 2:26

FOR the Apostles, Ascension day was one of subdued joy. Joy, because Jesus was going to the Father; subdued, because He was leaving them. There was about Olivet an air of quiet peacefulness. The Apostles were silent as Jesus blessed them, silent as He rose out of sight. They remained there in silence until two angels sent them off. "Jesus will come again, just as He ascended," in glory, in the clouds of heaven, surrounded by angelic armies. And what God has begun with the creation of the world, He will finish with the fullness of the coming of the Kingdom of God.

By the promise of Christ's second coming, I am assured of the triumph of God over evil.

III. THE DESCENT OF THE HOLY SPIRIT

"The light shines in the darkness, and the darkness has not overcome it."   *John 1:5*

IN God's Providence, "It's always darkest just before dawn." When the world was morally corrupt, the Christ Child came to save it. When the letter of the law had stifled the spirit of Jewish piety, Jesus came "that they might have life." While the apostles huddled together in an upper room, all their hopes in Jesus dashed by His death, the risen Lord appeared in the midst of them. And in the last days of the world, when "charity will grow cold" Jesus will restore all things to God.

"When it was dark, Jesus came unto them." When my soul is in darkness, God is at hand.

IV. THE ASSUMPTION OF OUR LADY INTO HEAVEN

"After speaking of the Church, her origin, mission and destiny, we can find no better way to conclude than by looking to Mary."

Catechism, no. 972

THE first book of the Old Testament tells of a woman who will crush Satan's head. In the last book of the New, St. John describes the great battle between a woman and Satan. The woman of Genesis is Mary; the sun-robed woman of the Apocalypse is the Catholic Church. Because Mary is the model of the Church one might understand the Church with a child in her womb is Mary at the Annunciation; the Church in travail is Mary on Calvary; the Church with twelve stars about her head is Mary at Pentecost, surrounded by the Apostles. And the Church with the moon at her feet is Mary assumed to heaven.

Mary is the Church's mother. I should ask her every day to protect the Mystical Body of her Son.

V. THE CORONATION OF THE BLESSED VIRGIN MARY

"There 'in glory of the most Holy and Undivided Trinity,' 'in the communion of all the saints,' the Church is awaited by the one she venerates as the Mother of her Lord and as her own mother."

Catechism, no. 972

"AND so from the Mount of Olives, they went back to the upper room and with one heart all joined constantly in prayer." And so the Acts of the Apostles tells us how you spent the last days of your life ... praying constantly.

You, the Mother of God, having watched Him ascend to the Father spent the rest of your life in prayer. You knew Jesus so well ... it is the way He spent His life, in prayer. Of course, you would do the same.

All of life, but especially the last days, are a good time to pray. A good time to be with God. A good time to spend with Mary and the Rosary.

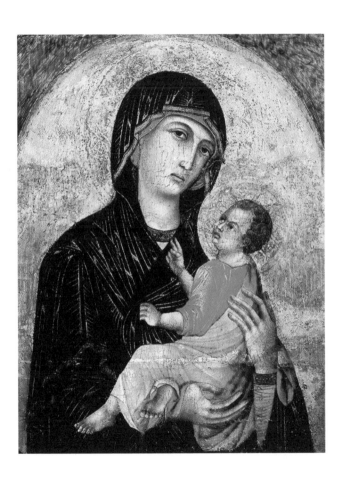

251

Personal Notes

The Joyful Mysteries

The Annunciation
The Visitation
The Birth of our Lord
The Presentation in the Temple
The Finding of the Child Jesus
    in the Temple

LOVE OF NEIGHBOR

Our Lady will give us a deeper understanding of
love of neighbor through the five Joyful Mysteries

—one—
Our Father, Who art in Heaven...
—ten—
Hail Mary, full of grace...
—one—
Glory be to the Father...

I. THE ANNUNCIATION

"I urge you to live in a manner worthy of the call you have received."

Ephesians 4:4

IT is well-nigh incredible; it staggers the human mind; but it is altogether true: God's love for us is infinite. That is the meaning of the Annunciation. God so loved the world, He sent Jesus to be our brother. After an eternity of waiting, God's love broke the bounds even of infinity; the Word was made flesh; God became one of us. This is our faith. Do I believe that God could love me that much? And if I do, what decisions do I need to make for today and the future?

Jesus lived His life for others. What does my neighbor need from me today?

II. THE VISITATION

*"Although I am free in regard to all, I have made
myself a slave to all so as to win over as many as
possible."*

1 Corinthians 9:19

AT first glance, Mary seems to have had a choice:
to stay at Nazareth and "love the Lord her God,"
newly conceived in her womb, or to "love her
neighbor" by visiting Elizabeth. Really, there was
no choice. One can choose only between two
separable things. The love of God and the love of
neighbor are the same; the one brings on, sustains
and requires the other. All love is a seamless robe.
Anyone who says "I love God," and does not love
his neighbor is a liar. Mary went to Elizabeth
because she loved her neighbor and, because she
loved God so much, she went in a hurry.

The way I treat others is the way I love God. It's
as uncomplicated as that!

III. THE BIRTH OF OUR LORD

"But I say to you: love your enemies and pray for those who persecute you." Matthew 5:44

WE are all sinners, which is why we ask who must I love? Who is my neighbor? Every human being is my neighbor. No sifting, sorting, selecting; love has a single eye. Jesus made no choice; He was born for those who loved Him and for those who didn't. He left angels and befriended publicans. He washed the feet of even those who betrayed Him. What uncalculating love, Christ's! And that love is a commandment.

To like everyone is impossible; but with Christ, I can love all, putting myself out to be kind to everyone.

IV. THE PRESENTATION IN THE TEMPLE

"She never left the temple but worshipped night and day with fasting and prayer."   *Luke 2:37*

ANNA was not merely noticed; she was studied. Everyone watched her. The Doctors of the Law were secretly grateful for her; she gave them self-confidence. For those who were – just as secretly – tired of the Doctors' tangled piety, Anna's fervor was a refreshing commentary on the marrow of the Law. She quietly put the proud Pharisees to shame; Anna had won a public without advertising. The pagans, restricted to the outer court, knew only of the Temple's "business," the loud interminable buying and selling; somehow, this woman's presence dignified even the outer court. Anna was, without a word, everybody's sermon.

Good example shines on the just and the unjust. It is one way for me to love everyone.

V. THE FINDING OF THE CHILD JESUS IN THE TEMPLE

"All who heard him were astounded."   Luke 2:47

IT was an uncomfortable three days for the Doctors. A small Boy telling them they'd been missing the point. Very courteously, and without saying it in so many words, and charmingly, without the bite of mercenary zeal, He told the teachers they didn't know the important things. As if they had been sitting there a lifetime looking at a fine dinner, talking about it, guessing the age of the wine, weighing each dish, reckoning the cost and debating the food value – and never eating it. And He was right. They knew He was right. Truth was in this Child who discussed religion with more than authority. He was authority!

Zeal is love outspoken. If I love others as Christ, I'll not just "keep the faith"; I'll spread it.

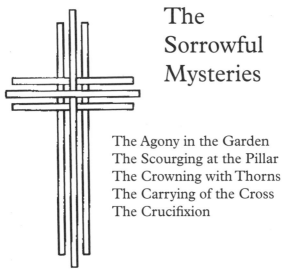

The Sorrowful Mysteries

The Agony in the Garden
The Scourging at the Pillar
The Crowning with Thorns
The Carrying of the Cross
The Crucifixion

CHRIST'S KINDNESS IN HIS PASSION

Our Lady will give us a deeper understanding of *Christ's kindness in His passion* through the five Sorrowful Mysteries

—one—
Our Father, Who art in Heaven...
—ten—
Hail Mary, full of grace...
—one—
Glory be to the Father...

I. THE AGONY IN THE GARDEN

"Jesus touched his ear and healed him."

Luke 22:51

WE might expect that Jesus would be so preoccupied with His sufferings on Good Friday that He would not have any time for anything else. The night before He had given Himself in the Eucharist; now He was giving His life. Surely that is enough "compassion on the multitudes." But no; even in His Passion, Jesus "went about doing good." In Olivet, He invited His disciples to share His agony with Him; when they slept, He forgave; He called Judas His friend; He ordered His captors to let the disciples go free; and with a touch, He healed the severed ear of Malchus, who had come to take Him captive.

Jesus did not omit little acts of kindness, even in His terrible suffering. That is the test of a loving heart.

II. THE SCOURGING AT THE PILLAR

"If I have spoken wrongly, testify to the wrong; but if I have spoken rightly, why do you strike me?"

John 18:23

THE mob had no difficulty with their divine Prisoner. They wished to kill Him, and He was willing to die; except in their motives, there was no conflict. When the high priest's servant slapped His face, Jesus shamed him with the gentlest possible reproach: "I spoke no evil. Why did you strike me?" When Peter denied Jesus three times, Peter wept. Jesus looked beyond his fear-based denial and saw the man to whom He would say, "feed my lambs." Judas would have been forgiven, too, but he judged his crime too great for Jesus to overlook. How little he understood the kindness of Christ!

To forgive is divine; Jesus proved that. I am most like Him when I act kindly towards those who have hurt me.

III. THE CROWNING WITH THORNS

"That day Herod and Pilate became friends."

Luke 23:12

GOD is so merciful that He does not begrudge earthly blessings even to the wicked. In our Lord's parable, Abraham called to the rich man across the chasm between heaven and hell: "In your lifetime you had many good things." That was the reward the rich man had set his whole heart on, and God allowed him to have it. Often, in exposing the hypocrisy of the Pharisees, Jesus remarked, "Amen, they have had their reward." And in His Passion, Jesus Himself was the instrument whereby two evil men, Herod and Pilate, became fast friends – "whereas before they had been enemies."

God is kind even to those who will have no part with Him, here or hereafter. He wants me to imitate Him.

IV. THE CARRYING OF THE CROSS

"On their way out they came across a man from Cyrene, Simon by name and enlisted him to carry his cross."

Matthew 27:32

THE journey up and down narrow, dusty streets from the Praetorium to Calvary must have been a nightmare for the worn-out Christ with a cross on His back. But Jesus was never too tired to console His friends. He filled the Cyrenean's heart with a strange, delightful peace and joy. Gently He told the mourning women to hold back their tears for their children. He left the image of His Face on Veronica's veil, repaying her sympathy with a miracle of thoughtfulness. And His Mother Mary found the strength to bear her sorrow in a glance from Her Son as He passed.

The fruit of suffering well borne is sensitivity to others who suffer. If I bear trials and pains patiently, as Christ did, I'll be kind and consoling to others, as Christ was.

V. THE CRUCIFIXION

"Amen, I say to you, today you will be with me in Paradise."   Luke 23:43

AT the summit of His suffering – His agony on the cross – Jesus simply radiated His divine mercy. While His enemies were pounding nails through His hands and feet, He forgave them, and prayed for their repentance. His first word on the up-raised cross was a promise of Paradise to His crucified companion who a short while before had reviled Him. Jesus gave Mary to John to be the whole world's dearest mother. And a moment before His death He cried out to His Father with a voice so mighty that the centurion, as if echoing that cry, was forced to confess: "Indeed, this man was the Son of God!"

Jesus, be as kind to me as You are to other sinners. And give me Your merciful heart.

The Glorious Mysteries

The Resurrection
The Ascension of our Lord
The Descent of the Holy Spirit
The Assumption of our Lady
    into Heaven
The Coronation of the Blessed
    Virgin Mary

THE SAME FOREVER

Our Lady will give us a deeper understanding
of Jesus Christ, *the same forever* through the five
Glorious Mysteries

—one—
Our Father, Who art in Heaven...
—ten—
Hail Mary, full of grace...
—one—
Glory be to the Father...

265

I. THE RESURRECTION

"And know that I am with you always; yes, to the end of time."   *Matthew 28:20*

IT is a fact that God created the world out of nothing; and it is a symbol as well. It is God's work; He reconciled us to Himself through Christ. St. Paul tells us that on the Cross, God the Father and Jesus, His Son, participated in the emptiness and brokenness of our human condition. As a result of that fact there will never be a dark corner of human suffering, pain or guilt that will be a sign of the absence of God.

The key to the Resurrection is understanding how incredible God's participation in the Cross is. It is the greatest kind of love.

Jesus, I believe you are with me in all my pain and sorrow. Alleluia!

II. THE ASCENSION OF OUR LORD

"So stay awake, because you do not know either the day or the hour."   *Matthew 25:13*

SPACE and time are no obstacles to Christ's loving care for souls. When He ascended into heaven, He disappeared from the Apostles' sight; but they did not vanish from His sight. Before the Son of God appeared among us as the divine Lamb of God, the Good Shepherd, the Light of the World, and the Way of Life, He had been in the bosom of the Father mercifully watching over the world. Can we understand how this is possible? Only in faith. Will we ever know why it happened, when it happened? Doubtful. Some things are God's business.

Lord, let me not be concerned about the things I cannot control. Before I leave this earth, Mary, help me accomplish what I was sent to do.

III. THE DESCENT OF THE HOLY SPIRIT

"Then they will hand you over to be tortured and put to death."   *Matthew 24:9*

THE Jewish patriarch Joseph was a living prophecy of Christ. He was his father's well-beloved son, innocent and holy. He loved his brothers but was hated by them and sold for twenty pieces of silver. He was imprisoned between criminals. He saved the lives of his brothers who had sold him. God might have said of Joseph what He would say of Jesus through the prophet Isaiah: "Behold! I lay in Zion a stumbling-block and a rock of scandal." He could say the same after Pentecost when the Apostles were scourged by the Sanhedrin for reminding them of Christ.

If I am "another Christ," as Joseph and the Apostles were, I may have to suffer for Him. Am I prepared?

IV. THE ASSUMPTION OF OUR LADY

"God loved the world so much that he gave his only Son."   *John 3:16*

THE philosophies and religions of antiquity had many names for God: First Cause, the Great Spirit. In the Old Testament, God tells Moses, *"I am who am."* Jesus, in the New Testament, tells us God is Father; God is Love. The Holy Spirit is the bond of love between Father and Son; that is, love makes God a Trinity. The world was born of this divine love. That same love drew Mary up to heaven as the apple of God's eye. Mary began to love her divine Son, and will never cease to love. But God never began to love. He always loved and always will, because Love is God.

Jesus Christ is divine Love Incarnate. God sent Jesus to teach us how to love Him.

V. THE CORONATION OF THE BLESSED VIRGIN MARY

"These are recorded so that you may believe that Jesus is the Christ, the Son of God, and that believing this may have life through his name."   *John 20:31*

JESUS' coming into the world opened up radically new possibilities of existence. Jesus came so we could see God in a totally new way. Jesus came to proclaim God's love for us as Abba.

Jesus continues to reveal God to us in many ways ... through the Church, through Scripture, through the world, nature and the people around us. Once we have experienced "Abba," we have a new understanding of the world, of ourselves and of other people.

Mary, your experience of God transformed you. Pray with me that I will be open to experiencing that same transforming grace – now and at the hour of death. Amen.

Personal Notes

271

Mysteries of Light

The Baptism in the Jordan
The Wedding at Cana
The Proclamation of the
Kingdom of God
The Transfiguration
The Institution of the
Eucharist

Introduction

In October 2002 the world welcomed the Apostolic letter, *Rosarium Virginis Mariae*, written by Pope John Paul II. In that letter he declared a year of the Rosary in which this traditional contemplative prayer would be especially emphasized and promoted.

Pope John Paul II's presentation of the Rosary as a prayer to "contemplate with Mary the face of Christ" gives encouragement to all Christians responding to the call of the Holy Spirit to "set out into the deep (*duc in altum!*)" in the third millennium.

To make this gift to the church even more significant during Pope John Paul II's 25th year as

Father John Phalen with Pope John Paul II.

the Vicar of Christ on earth, he suggested that the
Mysteries of Light be prayed on Thursdays by the
faithful. This proposed addition to the traditional
mysteries offers the opportunity to contemplate
the public life of Jesus and the affect of his teaching, healing and reconciling presence to people.
While it is the practice of the laity which will
ultimately determine the staying power of these
mysteries, the leadership of Pope John Paul II
supplementing the 15 mysteries with the
Mysteries of Light is welcomed enthusiastically by
those who, like Pope John Paul II, go to Jesus
through Mary. One cannot help but notice the

similarity between Pope John Paul II's *Totus Tuus* ("all yours") and Father Peyton's *"All for Her."*

Holy Cross Family Ministries offers here a series of reflections in the tradition of our founder, Servant of God Father Patrick Peyton, CSC. We encourage you to make use of these rich gospel scenes in your Thursday prayer and to change the use of the Joyful Mysteries to Saturday as well as the traditional Monday.

May this simple Rosary prayer which "marks the rhythm of human life" become the consistent contemplative family prayer in the new millennium. May we grow in knowing Christ by this holy practice, which can only gladden the heart of the Mother of God. May Christ be our light and may we who, at Pope John Paul II's urging, pray these new Mysteries of Light for families and for peace, be ourselves light for the world. In Christ, Son of God and Son of Mary.

Fr. John Phalen csc

Father John Phalen, CSC
President of Holy Cross Family Ministries
Father Peyton Center
518 Washington Street
N. Easton, MA 02356

Mysteries of Light

The Baptism in the Jordan
The Wedding at Cana
The Proclamation of the
    Kingdom of God
The Transfiguration
The Institution of the
    Eucharist

Our Lady will give us a deeper understanding of the following topics through the five Mysteries of Light:

THE HUMILITY OF JESUS

Let us pray that Jesus Christ will give us a deeper sense of humility through the five Mysteries of Light.

I. THE BAPTISM IN THE JORDAN

"Jesus came from Nazareth of Galilee and was baptized in the Jordan by John."   Mark 1:9

JESUS approached his kinsman, John, at the Jordan and submitted to baptism. John's first encounter with Him was at the Visitation of his mother by Mary. John receives Jesus as his mother Elizabeth did, recognizing Jesus as the salvation of the world. Jesus did not hold this over his friend John, but "Who, though he was in the form of God, did not regard equality with God something to be grasped." (Phil 2:6)

God, help me realize that the mission given me by virtue of my baptism is but a sharing in the mission of Christ and not my own will.

II. THE WEDDING AT CANA

"Woman, how does your concern affect me? My hour has not yet come."　　　　　*John 2:4*

JESUS submits to the will of His mother because of her compassion for their hosts. Though he may have been justified in not giving the community this sign at that particular time, he does so because of Mary's compassion and love for humanity. Jesus' humility in submitting to the request of Mary, and alleviating the embarrassment of their hosts, shows us that no matter is too small with which to approach Our Lord and His Mother.

God, grant me the wisdom to discern with a humble heart, that which is necessary to complete your will in the world.

III. THE PROCLAMATION OF THE KINGDOM OF GOD

"Blessed are the poor in spirit, for theirs is the kingdom of heaven."

Matthew 5:3

"POOR in spirit" means to be lowly and humble. Humility is a virtue because it helps us to see ourselves as we truly are. The humble have no delusions about self. Humble people know what they can do themselves and for what they must rely on God's help. It takes the grace of the Holy Spirit to discern the difference. Jesus knew who He was and leads us on a journey to discover our role in His mission.

O God, you have blessed us with the example of your Son, Jesus. Help us to see one another as we truly are, and respond to His call with courage and generosity.

IV. THE TRANSFIGURATION

". . . Coming down the mountain, Jesus said, 'Do not tell the vision to anyone until the Son of Man has been raised from the dead'."   Matthew 17:9

JESUS' transfiguration was a spectacular revelation to Peter, James and John. Yet Jesus did not want them to share the experience with others until He was to rise from the dead. Jesus' death and resurrection had to be experienced before the glory of his transfiguration could be revealed. Like them, we cannot understand the truth of Jesus unless we first experience his life, death, and resurrection.

God of the living, help us to see that our experiences in life are part of the glory of our transformation to come.

V. THE INSTITUTION OF THE EUCHARIST

"Then he poured water into a basin and began to wash the disciples' feet and dry them with the towel around his waist."

John 13:5

THE Liturgy of Holy Thursday celebrates two main actions of Jesus' Last Supper. The Liturgy of the Eucharist is one and the Washing of the Feet, the other. This beautiful liturgy illustrates the fulfillment of Jesus' command to "Do this in remembrance of me" and "You ought to wash one another's feet." This is the inauguration of our Eucharistic command to take, eat, drink, and serve one another.

O God, your son Jesus gave us Himself in the form of bread, wine, and service. Help us to be true followers of Him by sharing ourselves with one another as He did with us.

CHRIST WILL COME AGAIN!

Let us pray that Jesus Christ will give us a deeper appreciation of the fact that He will come in glory through the five Mysteries of Light.

I. THE BAPTISM IN THE JORDAN

"Behold, the Lamb of God, who takes away the sin of the world . . . now I have seen and testified that he is the Son of God."

John 1:29b, 34

JOHN the Baptist saw Jesus for who He really was from the very beginning of his life. In the Jordan, John knew Jesus offered us true release from all our sins. He saw the Holy Spirit come down like a dove and remain with Him. John sees Jesus as both a man and the Son of God. He sees, then, Jesus in His glory as the Second Person of the Trinity.

O Blessed Trinity, we long to see you face to face in heaven. Help us to see You in each person we meet here in life. Show us your face and we shall be redeemed.

II. THE WEDDING AT CANA

"Everyone serves the good wine first . . . but you have kept the good wine until now."

John 2:10

WINE symbolizes Christ's blood and water, baptism and new creation. From the waters of baptism arises the timeless miracle of Our Lord's self-sacrificing love. The miracle of the wine prepares the believer for the expectation of an eternal wedding banquet in heaven. The prospect of plenty for all is a constant in scripture and tells us that Christ's second coming will afford us with all we need to live eternally.

O Jesus, come in glory; give us the faith to believe in your providence when we share selflessly in generosity. Prepare our hearts now for the heavenly wedding feast of your promise.

III. THE PROCLAMATION OF THE KINGDOM OF GOD

"Blessed are you who are poor, for the kingdom of God is yours . . . Rejoice and leap for joy on that day! Behold, your reward will be great in heaven."

Luke 6: 20b, 23a

JESUS proclaims the Kingdom of God that begins now and leads us to eternity. A special place in this Kingdom is reserved for the poor, the *anawim*, who herald the triumph of the Kingdom with their simple witness. They do not rely on power or wealth, but only upon God's grace for their welfare. Mary's Magnificat announced this new day, and Jesus' proclamation of the Kingdom affirms God's new reign.

O Savior of all, help us to rely on you for what we need. Purify our hearts and minds and detach us from what the world values as essential. Our trust is only in You.

IV. THE TRANSFIGURATION

"And he was transfigured before them; his face shone like the sun and his clothes became white as light."
                                                                    Matthew 17:2

MATTHEW likens the face of Jesus to that of Moses on Mount Sinai. His transformed appearance is a foretaste of His Resurrection and Second Coming. On the mount of Transfiguration, the apostles see Jesus as He will be in the Kingdom of His Father. Because it is not yet time for His glorification, He cautions them not to tell anyone until "the Son of Man has been raised from the dead."

Risen Lord, we await your coming in glory on the last day. Help us to "be not afraid" in the terrible times before your coming, but to take comfort in you alone.

V. THE INSTITUTION OF THE EUCHARIST

"I shall not eat it again until there is fulfillment in the kingdom of God . . . I shall not drink of the fruit of the vine until the kingdom of God comes."

Luke 22:16,18

THE Eucharist is the sacrament of Christ's ongoing presence in the Church. It is both a sacrament for today and forever. In it, Christ is given to us as strength for the journey to the Kingdom and as a foretaste of the Kingdom itself. Jesus does not only initiate the Kingdom of God by His second coming, He has begun it already in His Resurrection. Together we proclaim in the Eucharist, "Christ has died! Christ has risen! Christ will come again!"

Eternal God, you have prepared a place for us in your Kingdom through the life, death and resurrection of your Son and our brother, Jesus Christ. Through his merits may we be made worthy children of your Kingdom and learn to live as He taught us. Maranatha! Come Lord Jesus!

THE CHURCH

Let us pray that Christ will grant us a greater appreciation for the Church as it promotes the Kingdom of God.

I. THE BAPTISM IN THE JORDAN

"This is my beloved Son, with whom I am well pleased."

Matthew 3:17

Our Lord's baptism by his kinsman, John, marks the beginning of his public ministry. It is this ministry that is offered us by the Spirit in our own Baptism into the Church. As members of the Church, we continue His ministry in our own place and time. As Jesus' brothers and sisters, God the Father, speaks of us too as His "beloved sons and daughters". Our baptism makes us other Christs for our own day.

Lord God, help me to accept my mission as priest, prophet and king as a baptised Christian. May I imitate You in doing the will of the Father.

II. THE WEDDING AT CANA

"His mother said to the servers, 'Do whatever he tells you.'"   *John 2:5*

In the Wedding Feast of Cana, Mary takes the initiative in the ministry of Her Son. She tells the servants, "Do whatever he tells you." Mary, the Mother of the Church, is telling us the same. What it means to be a follower of Jesus as Church is contained in His pilgrimage of ministry. Mary tells us to preach, heal, love and sacrifice as He did. As difficult as that may seem, following Him in His Church is the only way to freedom. We must do whatever he tells us.

Loving Christ, may I come to You often in prayer, alone and with other members of the Church in order to discern what it is You tell me to do.

III. THE PROCLAMATION OF THE KINGDOM OF GOD

But that you may know that the Son of Man has authority to forgive sins on earth, he said to the paralytic, 'I say to you, rise, pick up your mat, and go home.'

Mark 2:10-11

The Church, like Peter's house in Capernaum, is a house of healing. The Church's primary clients are the suffering, the poor, and sinners. It is to them that Jesus' message is most attractive. We have to admit, in our heart of hearts, that all of us are equally broken and that He, through the Church, offers us this same tender touch of healing. There are always those too blind, too self-righteous, to accept this healing, but Christ's Church offers it to all who come to Him in truth.

Dear God, never allow me to become too proud to admit my need for Your forgiveness and Your healing.

IV. THE TRANSFIGURATION

"While he was praying his face changed in appearance and his clothing became dazzling white."

Luke 9:29

Sometimes we are only capable of seeing Christ's Church in its institutional incarnation. But the Spirit grants us moments when we see the Church in all its true glory, as the Apostles saw Jesus on the mount. Seeing the Church as it really is, the Mystical Body of Christ victorious in heaven and on pilgrimage on earth, is an act of faith and trust in the Holy Spirit. It is this Spirit which inspires us to join ourselves in the greater and holier Church that most accurately represents the Body of Christ.

Spirit of God, transfigure me so that I become more like Christ, the Redeemer and Savior.

V. THE INSTITUTION OF THE EUCHARIST

"He loved his own in the world and he loved them to the end."   *John 13:1b*

On the night before He died, Jesus took the Bread, the Cup, and His life and offered it for us, forever. We eat the Bread, share the Cup, and wash each other's feet in His Name as symbols of His perpetual love for us. These ongoing sacraments of worship and service bring His ministry to life in our world. Through the Church, Christ's ministry is forever – a healing, forgiving presence in a broken world. This is the Church; this is the legacy of our Savior, Jesus the Christ.

O Jesus, may I never take the privilege of receiving You in the Eucharist for granted. May Your Body and Blood make us all a more faithful church community.

GOD'S LOVE FOR US

Let us pray that Christ will give us a deeper understanding of God's love for us through the five Mysteries of Light.

I. THE BAPTISM IN THE JORDAN

"This is my beloved Son, with whom I am well pleased."   *Matthew 3:17*

CHRIST descended into the waters of the Jordan River, the innocent one who became "sin" for our sake (2 Cor. 5:21). The heavens opened wide and the voice of the Father proclaimed him the beloved Son. Our prayer time, too, is an opportunity to rejoice that we are beloved of God, that "God so loved the world that he gave his only Son so that everyone who believes in him (sees his light) might not perish, but might have eternal life." (John 3:16) The Spirit descended on him to invest him with his mission.

Loving God, help me to realize that the mission vested in me by virtue of my baptism is based upon Your tremendous love for me.

II. THE WEDDING AT CANA

"His mother said to the servers, 'Do whatever he tells you.'"   *John 2:5*

IN the finding of the Child, Jesus, in the Temple, He had to be about the work of His Father, while His mother was upset that He could have done such a thing as to go missing. Now at Cana it is the mother of Jesus who prepares the way for His self-manifestation as the Christ. "Do whatever He tells you," she says confidently to the servers, implying that the hour of His self-manifestation had come. What love was felt by Son and mother for the bride and groom. This was the first of many signs, which revealed Christ's glory.

Loving God, teach me that there is no need or disappointment I may experience which does not stir You to compassion.

III. THE PROCLAMATION OF THE KINGDOM OF GOD

"But that you may know that the Son of Man has authority to forgive sins on earth, he said to the paralytic, 'I say to you, rise, pick up your mat, and go home.'"
                                                Mark 2:10-11

WHAT greater sign of God's loving mercy than the testimony of forgiveness of sins freely given? The people were scandalized that Christ would forgive sins, and yet amazed when He cured a paralytic, having first forgiven him. The forgiveness combined with the healing are signs of the true identity of the merciful Christ (cf. Mark 2:3-13).

O God, You are so loving that You grant me forgiveness of my sins through the sacramental reconciliation offered by Your Church. What a grace and blessing! May I never be too proud to seek conversion. Help me see in Christ the revelation of Your Kingdom of mercy and light.

IV. THE TRANSFIGURATION

"While he was praying his face changed in appearance and his clothing became dazzling white."

Luke 9:29

THOSE who are close to God in prayer have something different about their appearance. There is an aura about them, much like what is depicted as a luminous halo. The fact is, real deep prayer changes us and makes us more loving, more like the Christ. In this mystery we contemplate the Christ, transfigured and beaming, shining in splendor and holiness. The voice of the Father speaks once again and commands the apostles to listen to His chosen Son.

Loving God, help me to remember those mountain-top experiences of grace and favor in which Your presence was so obvious to me. May the luminous memory of them motivate me to listen to Your word even when I am uninspired.

V. THE INSTITUTION OF THE EUCHARIST

"He loved his own in the world and he loved them to the end."

John 13:1b

JESUS, at the last supper, gave Himself to his apostles as bread and wine transformed, and as service in the washing of their feet. He revealed Himself not only as master and teacher, but as the Christ as He encouraged them to imitate Him by washing each other's feet.

Real love manifests itself in service. Help us, O God, to know how to reach out to others and aid them. I am confident that such washing of the feet will help me realize how great is Your love for all Your sons and daughters. May we imitate Christ in service.

THE SACRAMENTS

Let us pray that families will grow in their sacramental life and will avail themselves to receive God's graces through the sacraments.

I. THE BAPTISM IN THE JORDAN

"This is my beloved Son, with whom I am well pleased."
Matthew 3:17

IN this mystery, Jesus begins His public ministry of service. He reveals to us what it means to be of service to others. As Christians, we begin our journey in faith at our baptism. Our parents, godparents and those who share their faith in loving service to others, nurture us in this faith. Each one of us is called to give examples of this loving service to others.

Lord our God, may we reflect on our own baptism, be reminded of the graces received and reach out in loving service to those in need.

II. THE WEDDING AT CANA

"His mother said to the servers, 'Do whatever he tells you.'"   *John 2:5*

IN this mystery, Jesus performs His first miracle by changing the water into wine. His mother tells the headwaiter listen to what He tells you to do. In our lives, we are called to listen to Jesus and to develop obedience to God's will in our lives by entering into a grace filled life. In so doing, we surrender our plans for those that God has put forth and turn our lives over to God.

Lord our God, as we listen to Your Son Jesus, may we grow in trust in Your plans for us in this life and respond with confidence to all that You ask of us. May we grow in truly understanding what it means to render service in Your name to those who are in need and to do so with a loving and gentle presence.

III. THE PROCLAMATION OF THE KINGDOM OF GOD

"But that you may know that the Son of Man has authority to forgive sins on earth, he said to the paralytic, 'I say to you, rise, pick up your mat, and go home.'"   *Mark 2:10-11*

IN this mystery, we hear about the forgiveness of sins, about healing and about the building of the Kingdom of God. As Christians, we are called to be forgiving of one another and to join together in building the Kingdom of God where everyone will know who Jesus is and will experience His healing and forgiveness in their lives.

Lord our God, may we always approach You for the forgiveness of our sins, the healing of the pain and hurt in our lives and by this grace filled encounter with You through the Sacrament of Reconciliation. May we rejoice in living a grace filled life with You and be able to contribute in a healthy way to the building of Your Kingdom here on earth.

IV. THE TRANSFIGURATION

"While he was praying his face changed in appearance and his clothing became dazzling white."

Luke 9:29

IN this mystery, the apostles were overcome by the appearance of Jesus. The apostles entered into a sacred place of prayer with Jesus that changed their lives forever. We are invited to enter into this sacred place every time we participate in the sacraments that are offered to us as a means of receiving God's graces and each time we set aside time for prayer. When we prayerfully receive the sacraments, we come before God as who we are and slowly, each time, we experience a little bit more of a change in ourselves that brings us closer to God. In the sacrament for the sick, we experience God's glory and possibly even physical or spiritual healing.

Lord our God, may we always find time to be before You in prayer. When we receive Your sacraments, may we become aware of Your presence in our lives and how our lives change when we stand before You without barriers.

V. THE INSTITUTION OF THE EUCHARIST

"He loved his own in the world and he loved them to the end."   *John 13:1b*

IN this mystery, we see Jesus revealing to us what it means to be of service to those around us in the name of the Lord. His humble act of washing the feet of His disciples calls us to cultivate this same attitude of humility as we conform ourselves to Christ through the reception of the Eucharist. Jesus gave of Himself throughout His entire life and even in His death. We are invited to receive Him in the Eucharist each time we receive Holy Communion, and so to become like Him in service to His people.

Lord our God, may we approach those around us with this same humility that You showed by washing the feet of Your apostles and always reveal Your presence whenever we render service to those in need. May the Sacrament of Holy Communion be a regular part of our daily life and by receiving Your Body and Blood may we grow in love for You.

FAMILIES

Let us pray for all families that Christ will grant us, through the five Mysteries of Light, a deep love and an appreciation of their need for spiritual enrichment.

I. THE BAPTISM IN THE JORDAN

"This is my beloved Son, with whom I am well pleased."   *Matthew 3:17*

THE Baptism of Jesus marked the beginning of His ministry, and His ministry was service to others. As He would say later, "I came not to be served but to serve." As family we are called to serve each other and thus to achieve holiness. As Jesus was called to serve and to seek justice so too are we called. From our service to family we gain the strength, love and support to extend ourselves to serve our community and the world. Our heavenly Father will be well pleased with us in our service to others.

O loving God, bless all families with unity and peace.

II. THE WEDDING AT CANA

"On the third day there was a wedding in Cana in Galilee and the Mother of Jesus was there."

John 2:1-12

THE fact that Jesus first revealed his power and purpose at a wedding has to be significant. It has to mean that marriage and family life are of primary concern to God. It has to mean that the work of healing and restoration begins with the marriage relationship and continues in the family. The quality of family life depends upon how well family members relate to one another. The small ways in which we appreciate and respect one another can do much to change the water of life into rich wine.

O God of the human family, strengthen all families in mutual love and faithfulness.

III. THE PROCLAMATION OF THE KINGDOM OF GOD

"And when he had said this, he breathed on them and said to them, 'Receive the Holy Spirit'..."

John 20:22-23

AT the baptism of Jesus, the Holy Spirit comes as a dove and signals the new spiritual beginning made possible by Jesus Christ. After the Resurrection Jesus breathes on the Apostles telling them to receive the Holy Spirit. At Pentecost the Spirit appears as tongues of fire.

As a dove, breath of God, fire, and wind, the Spirit appears. May we feel the loving energy and presence of the Spirit in our family. May we especially experience it in our moments of forgiveness and reconciliation and new beginnings.

O Holy Spirit, help us by Your guidance to realize the Kingdom of justice, peace and love proclaimed by Christ.

IV. THE TRANSFIGURATION

"While he was praying his face changed in appearance and his clothing became dazzling white."
                                        Luke 9:29

THE symbol of light is associated with Jesus throughout the liturgical year. He is called the Rising Sun, the Star of Morning and the Radiant One. In the Transfiguration Jesus is no longer represented as a symbol of light. Here we see Him as THE LIGHT. No lights are needed to illumine His way, for He is the light, unfading, unfailing, undying. Ask this Christ to light up our eyes and our ears, our hearts and minds that we might appreciate, in new light, our family. What can we see that is special about mother, father, sister, brother, and the elders in the family?

O Christ, enlighten and transfigure us and our families.

V. THE INSTITUTION OF THE EUCHARIST

"He loved his own in the world and he loved them to the end."

John 13:1b

EVERYTHING about the institution of the Eucharist speaks to us about self-giving and service. Jesus breaks the bread which is His Body and shares it with His friends. After He had washed the Apostles' feet, another sign giving in service to others, He put His cloak back on and reclined at table once more.

The table, the bread, the food prepared and eaten, the basins, the towels, the family members in need of our love and service, these are all reminders of the Eucharist. After Jesus washed the feet of the Apostles He said to them: "Do you understand what I just did for you?"

O Jesus, give us understanding and the determination to conform ourselves to You through emulating Your actions.

THE KINDNESS OF CHRIST

Let us pray that Christ will help us through the Mysteries of Light to experience His kindness in our lives.

I. THE BAPTISM IN THE JORDAN

"Here is the Lamb of God who takes away the sin of the world!"

John 1:29

JOHN'S life had been a study in gray. No doubt, at a tender age he was told that he was to be the prophet of the Messiah. John made his way to the desert where he prayed and fasted day and night. Under divine inspiration, he went forth to the river Jordan, where he preached the coming of the Messiah and baptized the poor in spirit.

Jesus, about to begin His own public life, stood before John, waiting to descend into the waters. John was given to recognize Him: "The Lamb of God! I should be baptized by you!" No, John, this is your hour, the climax of your life.

May we recognize Jesus as "The Lamb of God."

II. THE WEDDING AT CANA

"The mother of Jesus said to him, 'they have no wine.' And Jesus said to her, 'Woman, what concern is that to you and to me? My hour has not yet come." His mother said . . . 'Do whatever he tells you'."

John 2:3-5

MARY knew her Son, and knew instinctively when she could override His veto. She learned that lesson when she found Him as a Boy with the doctors in the temple, having lost Him for three agonizing days. She expostulated with Him. "Why, my Son, did you do this to your father and me?" He in turn expostulated with her. "I thought you knew I've come on my Father's business." She gently took His hand and He let her lead Him away.

He has infinite compassion for sinners and saints alike, yet He hides His kindness. He delays answering our prayers so that we can comfort ourselves with our persistence in begging for His help.

May our lives know the kindness of Jesus.

III. THE PROCLAMATION OF THE KINGDOM OF GOD

"Let the little children come to me . . . for it is to such as these that the Kingdom of heaven belongs."

Matthew 19:14

IN the silent film classic, "The King of Kings," there is a scene in which Jesus, as was His wont, is surrounded by the lame and the blind. Suddenly He stops and looks down. He sees a little girl smiling up at Him, as only a small child can. In one hand is her doll. In the other she holds the doll's arm, come undone from its body. He takes the doll from her "mother," takes a needle and a piece of goat's hair thread, sews the arm back on its body and returns it to the adoring child.

When was the last time you did something for someone? When was the last time someone did something for you? He is behind all the kindnesses of the world.

IV. THE TRANSFIGURATION

"And he was transfigured before them; his face shone like the sun and his clothes became dazzling light. Suddenly, Moses and Elijah appeared to them, talking with him."

Matthew 17:2-3

JESUS stands at the top of a high mountain. Peter, James and John keep their eyes on Him. Suddenly, Jesus erupts in dazzling light, and at the same moment two Israelite heroes – Moses, the fabled ruler of his people, and the prophet Elijah, the ruler of the people, appear beside Him and converse with Him about His coming Passion and death.

Peter, always the first to comment on Jesus' behavior, says, "Lord, it is good for us to be here!" With which, Moses and Elijah disappear, Jesus "comes down to earth," and, Jesus has once again shown His kindness to His apostles.

As for us, we await the invitation of Jesus to enter the Promised Land forever.

V. THE INSTITUTION OF THE EUCHARIST

"I tell you, before the cock crows you will have denied me three times."

John 13:36,38b

JESUS: "Where I am going you cannot go now, but later you will go."
Peter: "Why cannot I go with you now? I am ready to die for you!"
Jesus: "Are you ready? I tell you, tonight before cockcrow, you will deny me three times."

What if this exchange between Jesus and Peter had not taken place? He would not have noticed the cock's crowing; he would be immersed in his guilt. In despair, he had abandoned Jesus. So Jesus, knowing all the possibilities, told Peter the harsh truth of his betrayal. Never were kinder words spoken, but then Jesus can never say anything harsh without His divine love shining through.

Something for me to remember whenever He suggests, through others, that I am not the Christian I think I am.

THE FATHER'S VIEW OF JESUS

Let us pray that Christ may bring us to a deeper understanding of the Father's view of Jesus through the Mysteries of Light.

I. THE BAPTISM IN THE JORDAN

"I saw the Spirit descending from heaven like a dove, and it remained on him."   *John 1:32*

SOME day Jesus would be Christ the King of Heaven and Earth. You wouldn't suspect that if you saw Him before John the Baptist, lowering Himself into the waters of the Jordan, symbolically dying to sin and then rising. No one in the crowd of onlookers looked twice at Jesus.

That is, until John spoke out in a thunderous voice, "I saw the Spirit come down like a dove from heaven and rest on Him. And in His turn, God the Father opened His heart as He proclaimed, 'You are my own dear Son. I am well pleased with you'."

Father, let me see Jesus as you see Him. And Jesus, meek and humble of heart, make my heart Thine.

II. THE WEDDING AT CANA

"The mother of Jesus said to him, 'They have no wine.' [And] Jesus said to her, 'Woman, how does your concern affect me? My hour has not yet come'. His mother said to the servers, 'Do whatever he tells you.'"

John 2:3-5

THE Mother of Jesus was invited, as were Jesus and His disciples, to a wedding at Cana. Mary brought bad news to Jesus. "They have no wine."

"What is that to us? My time has not yet come." Mary was asking for a miracle; Jesus was doing what He was best at, leading her to greater trust in Him. Mary responded to one of the waiters, "Do whatever He tells you." Jesus smiled at His mother and asked the waiter to fill some earthen pots with water. That done, "Now bring a glass of it to the steward." The steward said, "You've saved the best wine till now!"

Jesus would often say to His disciples, "The good you do, do secretly and your Father, who sees you in everything will repay you."

III. THE PROCLAMATION OF THE KINGDOM OF GOD

"Do not think I have come to abolish the law or the prophets; I have come not to abolish but to fulfill."

Matthew 5:17

JESUS came to change water into wine, the dead to life, bread and wine into Himself; in short, to befriend sinners and change them into saints.

He does it on every page of the Gospels. He knew precisely what is in mankind: the good and the bad, the wheat and the tares, the sheep and the goats, the heaven and the hell. What He was looking for in the men and women He met was not their failings, but their potential. Anything at all that He could grasp and use to their advantage. Jesus' life was spent calling sinners and actualizing saints. He treated no two alike. He knew where all of them, all of us, were coming from.

Let us joyfully call ourselves what we are, sinners – that the fullness of Jesus may dwell in us. Amen, so make it be.

IV. THE TRANSFIGURATION

". . . Jesus took with him Peter and James and his brother John and led them up to a high mountain by themselves."

Matthew 17:1

THERE is no question but that Jesus played favorites. Mary, Joseph, The Baptist, the apostles, dozens more throughout His earthly life. He was perfectly human and behaved much like any of us when it came to choosing intimate friends, or doing good to those whom He knew would be grateful for His help, even for His rescuing.

Each one of us has moments with Jesus that are unique to ourselves; bright spots in our dull days, as the transfiguration was to the apostles.

Yes, Jesus had His special friends. But more importantly He was a special friend to His Father, who directed Him to a mountaintop to share His splendor with His best friends. And Jesus is special, not only to His Father, but to each of us.

And if we want it so, Moses and Elijah can become close to us in our prayer.

V. THE INSTITUTION OF THE EUCHARIST

"Unless I wash you, you will have no inheritance with me."

John 13:8

IT has been a solemn, thought provoking Passover meal for the apostles under the guidance of Jesus' providence. He had occasioned their wonderment and Peter's scandal by kneeling before each in turn and washing their feet. Suddenly He groaned, revealing to them that one of their number was on the point of betraying Him to the watchful authorities. He gave His guests, and us, a new commandment: "As I have loved you, so you must love one another." He promises them the Holy Spirit to finish in them what Jesus has so well begun. He calls them fruitful branches of the true vine Himself.

An hour later, the Jesus who had poured out His heart to His friends, was begging His Father to take His coming Passion from Him if at all possible. An angel, sent by the Father, came to console Him.

FORGIVENESS

Let us pray for an experience of God's forgiveness in our lives through the Mysteries of Light.

I. THE BAPTISM IN THE JORDAN

"I am baptizing you with water, for repentance, but the one who is coming after me is mightier than I."
                                                                                    Matthew 3:11

THE witness to the baptism of Jesus in the Jordan reveals the power of our loving God in our lives when it comes to the forgiveness of sins. Through our baptism we have been freed from original sin and given the grace to follow in the footsteps of our Savior. Each time we renew our baptismal promises we recall our commitment to reject Satan and all his works and to believe in the Good News. Each time we make the sign of the cross with the holy water as we enter or leave the church, we are reminded that we have been baptized with water and the Holy Spirit and called by name to follow Jesus Christ.

Lord Jesus, help us through this reflection on Your baptism, to always be ready to ask for forgiveness when we have fallen from a grace filled life.

II. THE WEDDING AT CANA

"And Jesus said to her, 'Woman, how does your concern affect me? My hour has not yet come.'"

John 2:4

IN this the first of Jesus' public miracles, we hear that there is no more wine. Imagine that you are at a wedding and are told there is no more wine. The embarrassment of the bridegroom's family to have their guests without wine is an experience that many do not wish to live. Words asking forgiveness must have uttered out of their mouths. There are times when we find ourselves in those self-conscious moments when we need to ask for pardon or to say, "I'm sorry" to those whom we love. Jesus teaches us not to panic and how to live in a spirit of forgiveness.

Lord Jesus, may we turn to You in our moments of embarrassment and learn how to respond in a loving and forgiving way.

III. THE PROCLAMATION OF THE KINGDOM OF GOD

"Child, your sins are forgiven."

Mark 2:5

JESUS says to the paralyzed man, "Your sins are forgiven .... Rise, pick up your mat and walk." To the scribes Jesus was blaspheming, for they believed that no one had the power to forgive sins but God. Yet Jesus knew exactly what they were thinking and challenged them. Through this mystery, we are invited to examine our lives and place before God the areas that need healing from our brokenness and forgiveness from our sinfulness.

Lord Jesus, may we experience the power of Your healing and forgiving presence to each of us, paralyzed as we are by sinfulness and brokenness.

IV. THE TRANSFIGURATION

"As he spoke, a cloud came and covered them with a shadow; and when they went into the cloud the disciples were afraid."

Luke 9:34

THE disciples were invited by Jesus to go with Him to the mountaintop to pray and to spend some special time with Him. Peter, James and John were afraid when they began to experience something unknown to them. Jesus loved His friends and showed great patience with them yet He was firm in telling them they could not stay together on the mountaintop. During His life, Jesus experienced many moments of forgiveness with His friends, especially with Peter. In prayer, we have moments when we are afraid, for we do not know where God is leading us, yet we desire to follow with our hearts.

Lord Jesus, as we experience some unknown places in our lives, may we be as forgiving with our close friends as You were with Your friends.

V. THE INSTITUTION OF THE EUCHARIST

"At the moment you do not know what I am doing, but later you will understand."

John 13:7

PETER did not want Jesus to wash his feet. Jesus in his compassion for Peter said, "If I do not wash you, you can have nothing in common with me." At that, Peter said, "wash all of me." Peter witnesses to us what happens when we seek to occupy the high ground and fail to recognize our own needs. Peter once again learns a severe lesson about the compassion and forgiveness in his relationship with Jesus. We need to learn from Peter how to include ourselves among the sinful and humble children of God.

Lord Jesus, may we experience Your compassion and forgiveness especially when we are uncertain about events that have happened in our lives that have led us to stray from Your grace.

SERVICE IN THE CHURCH

Let us pray that Christ will teach us how and why we are called to service in the Church through the Mysteries of Light.

I. THE BAPTISM IN THE JORDAN

"Allow it now, for thus it is fitting for us to fulfill all righteousness."   *Matthew 3:15*

JESUS was standing in line to be baptized by John. When it came time for Him to be baptized John said, "It is I who need baptism from you." We are all in need of God's graces to remain focused on the events in our lives that call us to be of service to those around us. We can sense that we are not worthy to become involved in a certain ministry, but Jesus reveals for us the gifts that are given us in order to render this service to which we are called. Like John, we are called to live sacred moments despite our feelings of unworthiness.

Jesus, we ask that You continue to bless us with a deeper understanding of those moments when we are called to live in humility as we answer the needs of our Church.

II. THE WEDDING AT CANA

"Fill the jars with water."

John 2:7

JESUS in His relationship with His mother reveals for us the unique bond between a parent and child. Many times we are asked to do something that does not seem logical and we ask why. Jesus asks the waiter to fill the jars with water. Perhaps an odd request and one that the waiter would have preferred not to complete. We are perhaps asked by family members or coworkers to complete tasks that do not seem too practical or logical and would rather debate their relevance. Jesus, in His first miracle, reveals for us a trust level that comes as we reflect on our understanding of the call to serve God in our lives.

Lord Jesus, give us the grace to discern what is being asked of us at this moment.

III. THE PROCLAMATION OF THE KINGDOM OF GOD

"I say to you, rise, pick up your mat, and go home."

Mark 2:11

IN this story the house Jesus is in becomes very messy. As we grow closer to Jesus and we become more aware of the needs of those around us; our lives become complicated and so much more is demanded of us. This is true of the man whose house Jesus is in. Four people knew how important it was for their sick friend to see Jesus that they make a hole in the roof of the house. Jesus heals the man by forgiving his sins and making him physically sound again. When we allow Jesus into our homes, our lives become messy but so much more complete.

Jesus, may we always welcome You into our homes and be ready to serve those who desire to come close to You.

IV. THE TRANSFIGURATION

"They fell silent and did not at that time tell anyone what they had seen."

Luke 9:36

PETER, James and John went with Jesus to the mountaintop to pray. Their experience was one of great joy in that they were with Jesus in a sacred moment in life. Yet, after this experience, they were so moved by emotion that they could not speak. We, too, have moments when we find ourselves on the mountaintop and do not want to come down. These moments can be with good friends, co-workers or family members and we are so affected by this personal witness that our lives are changed forever.

Jesus, as we become aware of our experiences on the mountaintop, may we be motivated to radiate this love of God to all those whom we serve in our daily lives.

V. THE INSTITUTION OF THE EUCHARIST

"I have given you a model to follow, so that as I have done for you, you should also do."

John 13:15

WHEN we look at the example that Jesus has given us in the washing of the feet at the Last Supper, we are reminded of our need to witness the simplicity and humility of Jesus in everything that we do. There are events that may appear to be so small and insignificant that we forget that Jesus has given us an example to follow that touches every single aspect of our lives; from giving a simple cup of water to a thirsty person to being present with someone who is preparing to enter into eternal life. Whatever we do to the least of our friends we do to Jesus.

Lord Jesus, in our call to serve the needs of those around us, may we be mindful that we are doing everything for Your glory.

Personal Notes

Personal Notes

Our Mission

In the spirit of our founder, Father Patrick Peyton, CSC, and under the sponsorship of the Congregation of Holy Cross, **Holy Cross Family Ministries** serves Jesus Christ and His Church throughout the world by promoting and supporting the spiritual well-being of the family.

Faithful to Mary, the Mother of God, **Family Rosary** and **Family Rosary International** encourage family prayer, especially the Rosary.

Family Theater Productions directs its efforts to the evangelization of culture using mass media to entertain, inspire and educate families.

The **Father Peyton Family Institute** focuses on research and education in family life ministry and the relationship of spirituality to family.

HOLY CROSS
FAMILY MINISTRIES

Family Rosary
Family Theater Productions
Father Peyton Family Institute
Family Rosary International

518 Washington Street
North Easton, MA 02356-1200
Inside U.S.: 800-299-7729
Outside U.S.: 011-508-238-4095
www.hcfm.org

822833OB033E